Praise for *The Islamist Phoenix* (2014)

The Islamist Phoenix is a great entry point for those in want of a more solid understanding of the history and social complexities involved in the rise of the Islamic State. Loretta Napoleoni explains how this iteration of Islamism does not form from a vacuum, but almost inevitably, and sometimes knowingly, from the circumstances and conditions of the West's recent involvement in the Middle East in the last century. The Islamic State can, and almost certainly will, be defeated. But, how it is defeated is what truly matters, especially in the years, decades, and centuries to come.

Chelsea Manning

A vital contribution to our understanding of what is happening in the Middle East.

Chris Hedges

T0163231

Praise for *Terror Incorporated* (2005)

This thoughtful and incisive inquiry yields much insight into some of the most important issues of today, and tomorrow.

Noam Chomsky

A masterpiece ... This book should be required reading for everyone in the White House, State Department, and Pentagon.

Greg Palast, author of the New York Times bestseller *The Best Democracy Money Can Buy* and *The Jokers Wild: Dubyas Trick Deck* playing cards

NORTH KOREA

THE COUNTRY WE LOVE TO HATE

Loretta Napoleoni is the bestselling author of *Maonomics*, *Rogue Economics*, *Terror Incorporated* and *Insurgent Iraq*. She is an expert on terrorist financing and money laundering, and advises several governments and international organisations on counter-terrorism and money laundering. Napoleoni is a regular media commenatator for CNN, Sky and the BBC, and writes for *El Paris*, *The Guardian* and *Le Monde*. She lectures regularly around the world on economics, terrorism and money laundering.

LORETTA NAPOLEONI

NORTH KOREA

THE COUNTRY WE LOVE TO HATE

UWA PUBLISHING

First published in 2018 by
UWA Publishing
Crawley, Western Australia 6009
www.uwap.uwa.edu.au

UWAP is an imprint of UWA Publishing
a division of The University of Western Australia

 A catalogue record for this book is available from the National Library of Australia

Cover design by tendeersigh
Typeset in Bembo by Lasertype
Printed by Lightning Source

 uwapublishing

To Edi Bee

Contents

Introduction

Orientalist Bigotry

To many, North Korea is an aberration. It is considered the antithesis of democracy: a totalitarian regime, ruled by a dictatorial dynasty that successfully reinvented feudalism. The Democratic People's Republic of Korea (DPRK) is also unique. It has survived the implosion of the Soviet Union and the modernisation of Chinese communism – its northern neighbours and historical sponsors – without even the slightest attempt to open up to the West. But these facts alone do not fully capture the true nature of the country.

Nicknamed the hermit state, North Korea is so secretive that separating fact from fiction is often problematic. Indeed, the mystery surrounding this country has proven advantageous for other nations. In the post–Cold War era, the DPRK has allowed us to regard it as the ultimate dystopian society, an evil benchmark against which the spreading of democracy always appears positive.

Even Iraq or Libya are perceived as better regimes than The Democratic People's Republic of Korea (DPRK)!

North Korea is the enemy we all love to hate.

Yet, for all the comfort this statement may bring, it fails to comprehensively describe the North Korean regime or to address the fundamental question: how do we deal with it? The truth is that the DPRK is different: it does not fit neatly into any political classifications but, at the same time, displays features of several of them. Westerners have always rejected such complexity in an Asian country, choosing to label North Korea as another brutal communist regime. After the fall of the Berlin Wall, the entire world has embraced this interpretation.

Putting aside any form of oriental bigotry and avoiding well-known stereotypes, this book will try to present a dispassionate picture of The Democratic People's Republic of Korea while seeking to unveil why and how it has survived against all odds. Hopefully, this analysis will offer the reader some tools to begin to unravel the true nature of the hermit state, the first step to peacefully resolving the current situation.

Let's begin with North Korea's new young leader, Kim Jong-un. Parachuted into power in 2011 by the sudden death of his father, Kim Jong-il, the young Kim has attempted to merge the past with the future in order to lead the nation through a problematic present. This is not an easy task. Using the instruments of propaganda and economic innovation, Kim Jong-un has embarked on a masterplan to strengthen his legitimacy, proving to the people that he is fulfilling the same role as his grandfather, Kim Il-sung – in other words, that he is their sole protector.

Brushing aside the harsh memories of his father's ruling – from the famine of the late 1990s to the corruption of the elites – Kim has been reconnecting North Koreans with their glorious past: the long struggle of the war of independence, the birth of the new nation and the reconstruction after the Korean War. He is boosting the nation's pride. To speed this up, he has played on his physical resemblance to his grandfather. He has cut his hair in the same style and gained some weight, he dresses in a similar fashion and he even walks and laughs as Kim Il-sung did. This is a smart move. Veneration for the founder of the nation is genuine among the majority of North Koreans and the trick of presenting himself as the physical reincarnation of Kim Il-sung has boosted the popularity of the new leader, who was relatively unknown just seven years ago.

Putting aside these clever techniques to consolidate his power, Kim Jong-un has a distinctive vision of the world, different from his grandfather's and his father's. Unlike Kim Il-sung who fought colonialism or Kim Jong-il who grew up during the Cold War, Kim Jong-un is a millennial and understands the meaning of globalisation. He knows it will be harder and harder to keep the world at bay, while also sensing that relying on the traditional Cold War dichotomy, so dear to his grandfather and father, could backfire. To survive the country needs to grow economically; this has been his message since the beginning.

Economic modernisation is indeed taking place in North Korea, but in a different fashion to that experienced in other totalitarian Asian countries, such as China. North Korea does not have a clear plan of economic modernisation. On the contrary, Kim Jong-un has shown a high degree of tolerance vis-à-vis the liberalisation of the economy, leaving this process in the hands of the people. Perhaps this is intentional as the central government could clamp down on informal markets at any time. More likely, this sort of *laissez-faire* approach constitutes a form of *juche* economics. North Korea has never truly relied on central planning, as the Soviet Union or China did, and has always shown a degree of 'uncertainty' about the future, which has provided it the necessary flexibility to survive major crises, such as the implosion of the Soviet Union. This is an important point.

The geopolitics of the globalised world are profoundly different from those of the colonial era and of the Cold War, with multipolarity replacing the classic dichotomy of the second half of the twentieth century. Born in the early 1980s, Kim Jong-un witnessed this transformation while growing up. That North Korea has at its helm someone who understands and accepts this new reality, coupled with the built-in flexibility of the North Korean system, is a distinct advantage.

Kim Jong-un, the millennial, has accelerated the nuclear program, investing in it heavily and dismissing as a deterrent the regular army, which he considers weak and somehow obsolete. The verbal confrontations with Donald Trump, Shinzo Abe and the South Koreans are pure propaganda. Kim Jong-un has no intention of bombing anybody, but he does want to prove that he could. Of course, as always in history, the final outcome will depend on variables that nobody can fully predict, Donald Trump being one of those, but it looks increasingly likely that The Democratic People's Republic of Korea will succeed in becoming a nuclear power despite breaking all the rules, as Pakistan did. At that point the only way to contain it will be to welcome Pyongyang into the nuclear club of nations. This membership will guarantee the survival of the regime in the near future. China, the regional and world giant on the northern border, is not hostile to this development. And this is what really matters.

The world we live in is very different from the one inhabited by Kim Il-sung, but it is also very different from the world at the beginning of the new millennium, before the birth of virtual life. Holding on to absolute power without any form of consensus is impossible. To illustrate this point we can draw a parallel between Kim Jong-un and another millennial, Saudi crown prince Mohammed Bin Salaman. The crown prince was not parachuted into power after a very brief period of time, but his rise to the top position has been equally exceptional and unexpected. Both young men have purged the old guard and present themselves as anti-corruption leaders. They have cut the old branches of power to send a strong message to all their subjects: I am here to rule, so do not mess with me. Such bold moves require confidence and support from within the ruling elite. The success of Kim Jong-un in holding power for so long seems to prove that he has been able to secure such backing.

Mohammed Bin Salaman also plays on his physical resemblance to his grandfather, the founder of Saudi Arabia, King Abdullahziz Ibn Saud, the man whose fifty-one year reign he may one day emulate. Presenting himself as the reincarnation of his grandfather is a technique to gain consensus, helped along by promises to bring about much-needed reforms. Economics is paramount – ending Saudi Arabia's dependency on oil – as is tolerance. While in the second half of 2017, his father allowed women to drive, possibly under his suggestion, the crown prince went as far as calling for a return to moderate Islam and to a tolerant society. The sharp departure from those who have ruled before him enhances the image of the crown prince as a ruler who will leave as deep an impression as King Abdullahziz. For many, Saudi Arabia is also an aberration because it is an absolute monarchy resting on feudal principles. But, as with North Korea, Saudi Arabia has shown a remarkable resilience, avoiding even the strong winds of the Arab Spring. Both countries are set to be ruled for decades to come by young millennial leaders who are very much the product of the authoritarian and brutal regimes they were born into. The sooner we realise this, the sooner we can begin working towards a new world order.

Prologue

Missile Crisis by Candlelight

On 13 February 2017, Donald Trump hosted a candlelit dinner for Japanese Prime Minister Shinzo Abe at his country club resort Mar-a-Lago, in Florida. As the guests were served the first course, the news came that North Korea had launched a test missile. Soon images surfaced on Facebook of the American and Japanese staff bringing documents for the two leaders to read by iPhone flashlight at their table. Too bad that the following day these historic photos were taken down.[1]

Abe and Trump, along with the private citizens attending the state dinner, continued their meal as the missile crisis unfolded, in the background the keyboard vocalist hired for the night sang on. For the Mar-a-Lago guests, the $200,000 they had paid to attend the state dinner proved to be a great investment; not only had they witnessed an international nuclear crisis live, some of them had even been able to take a selfie with the presidential military aide carrying the 'football', the black leather satchel containing the codes, manuals and equipment that are all that Trump needs to order a nuclear strike.[2]

Some people realised the significance of the missile launch, timed as the leaders of the two most important enemies of North Korea – Japan and the USA – shared their first official meal. Few understood the finesse with which Kim Jong-un, the grandson of Kim Il-sung, exacted his personal revenge.

As the American historian Bruce Cumings wrote, 'Abe is the grandson of Kishi Nobusuke, who was a war criminal, a Class A war criminal in World War II, according to the US occupation, and had been one of the people fighting against Kim Il-sung in Manchuria in the 1930s. He was responsible for munitions production.'[3] Abe's grandfather was released by the Americans after three years in prison and rehabilitated as an anti-communist. So you had the grandsons of two men who fought each other about eighty years ago confronting each other during a state dinner hosted by the president of the United States, the country responsible for the mutilation of the Korean peninsula at the end of the Japanese colonisation and South Korea's strongest ally.

The tests of four simultaneous missiles at the beginning of Donald Trump's term as president were also a direct response to the deployment of the THAAD anti-missile system in South Korea, which became operational in May 2017, for which the USA had hurried shipment to have the missiles in place before a progressive South

Korean president took over. Indeed, on 9 May 2017, the democratic party candidate, Moon Jae In, a human rights lawyer who favours dialogue with North Korea, won the election.[4]

With these tests, North Korea revealed to its enemies and to the world that it possesses nuclear capabilities heretofore undetected.

Chapter 1

Going Hungry

China and North Korea emerged from the ashes of World War II as the countries we think we know today. For decades after the end of the war, hunger and starvation plagued both nations, with famine one of the high costs of independence from colonisation – China's from European powers and Korea's from imperial Japan. Yet the intimate relationship between these two countries and peoples goes back well before modern history.

From its founding tens of centuries ago, Korea adopted the Chinese ideograph system and used Chinese characters in writing and literary language; until the fifteenth century the commonly spoken language was Korean. Korean society also imported Buddhism, a non-dogmatic religion that was quickly absorbed into local beliefs and superstitions.[1] But the solid bridge between the two cultures has always been Confucian philosophy. Stressing filial piety, loyalty to the ruler and harmonious order, Confucianism greatly influenced Korean social life, reinforcing its rigid form of feudalism. Just as the law of Rome was encoded into the system of values of Britain, wrote Reginald Thompson, a well-known British archaeologist,[2] so too the Chinese value system was engraved in Korean society.

China, therefore, is a useful tool with which to begin understanding North Korea. A common denominator is a strong national identity expressed through shared ethnicity, language and geographical boundaries, characteristics that have been in place for millennia in both nations. But, unlike China, Korea never experienced frequent and strong revolutionary outbursts, as it lacked the vibrant social engine that produced the unique Chinese political system of alternate dynasties. In comparison to China and throughout history, Korea was stagnant. That explains how one dynasty, the Choson, ruled the country from 1392 until Japan colonised the Korean peninsula at the beginning of the twentieth century.

Korean society was structured according to a rigid class system regulated by strictly hereditary principles; there was no social mobility. At the top of the social pyramid were the aristocrats, the *yangban*, who owned the land and had exclusive access to politics. At the bottom was a vast class of slaves, as Korea had one of the oldest and most longstanding systems of chattel slavery. Slaves were the property of the aristocracy and could be bought, sold, traded or inherited. They could be abused, branded, bred, exploited or killed by their owners. Through the centuries, slaves remained a constant feature of the Korean economy, ranging from 30 to 60 per cent of the population; in Seoul, where the elite gathered for socialising, business or politics, slaves outnumbered free people. Slavery in Korea was abolished in 1894. Between these two classes of aristocrats and slaves were the ordinary people, primarily peasants, artisans and labourers.

The rigid feudal class division is at the root of the fratricidal conflict that plagued the Korean peninsula in the first half of the twentieth century. When the imperial Japanese forces imposed colonial rule on Korea in 1910, the Korean aristocracy defended their own privileges, but not the nation. As a result, aristocrats morphed into a pro-Japanese ruling class located predominantly in the south. They became colonial officers in their ancestral lands, maintaining order in the southern regions, known as the rice basket of Korea, to guarantee a steady flow of rice to Japan. The north, rich in mineral and other natural resources, never accepted Japanese rule.

Victim of History
Colonisation arrived when Korea was experiencing positive changes. At the end of the nineteenth century, not even this feudal country was immune to the winds of modernisation. From commerce to music to literature and art, innovation swept through the Korean peninsula. Buddhism was joined by Christianity,[3] contributing to a tolerant approach vis-à-vis religion. In the north, this renaissance produced a new but small enlightened and entrepreneurial elite, which many believe could have successfully led the country into the twentieth century

and shaped the modern state of Korea. One can only speculate what would have happened if Korea hadn't been colonised by its neighbour: the effervescent Korean bourgeoisie might have even ended the rigid feudal structure. But Korea was colonised. The anti-colonial movement of 1919 was violently repressed, the 1920s witnessed the erosion of the traditional values and virtues of Korean society, and then in 1929 came the big crash. These factors sealed Korea's destiny.

The Great Depression triggered a predatory form of colonisation at the hands of the Japanese, whose entrepreneurial class had been destroyed by the 1929 crash. Poverty, hunger and famine grew throughout the peninsula and political persecution became rampant. To assimilate the country into the Japanese empire, Japan even began to systematically eradicate Korean national identity and culture – for example, Japanese names replaced Korean names and ancient artworks were destroyed or expatriated to Japan.[4]

During this period, a growing number of Koreans moved to the north, to Manchuria in China where, throughout the 1920s, the anti-Japanese resistance had relocated. Among these émigrés was the family of the future North Korean leader, Kim Il-sung.

Born on 15 April 1912, the day the *Titanic* sank in the Atlantic ocean, the future Kim Il-sung was given the name of Kim Song-ju. He was born in a village near Pyongyang, which at the time a budding commercial centre with a strong presence of American missionaries. His parents were Christians and belonged to the upwardly mobile middle class that had emerged in the early years of the twentieth century. They came from the Seoul-Kaesong-Pyongyang region of rich alluvial rice paddies and progressive urbanisation. In 1923 Kim Il-sung's father, who opposed the Japanese presence in Korea, was arrested for anti-Japanese activities. In 1925, soon after his release, he took the family to Manchuria, where he died a few years later. Escaping the Japanese empire, however, proved to be impossible for Kim's family: in 1931, Tokyo invaded Manchuria.

Japan separated the Manchurian region from China and created its own puppet state, Manchukuo. The Japanese population welcomed the conquest of Manchuria as its rich resources were soon tapped into by the badly bruised Japanese economy. Indeed, throughout the 1930s, Manchuria proved essential to Japan's economic recovery from the Great Depression. But ruling Manchuria was not easy. The Chinese, Russian and Korean ethnic populations organised a strong resistance against what many described as a brutal regime.

Indeed, the Japanese conducted a systematic campaign of terror and intimidation against the local population, involving arrests and executions. Because the Japanese army used Manchukuo as a base from which to invade the rest of China, soon the region became the theatre of one of the most vicious conflicts during World War II, involving several ethnic groups, among them Chinese, Russians and a vast number of Korean immigrants.

Across the border in Korea, the 1930s proved as traumatic a period as in Manchuria. By the beginning of 1939, over five million Koreans had become labourers for the Japanese and tens of thousands of men had been conscripted into the Japanese military machine. The Japanese forced approximately 200,000 girls and women, mostly from China and Korea, into sexual slavery for the military. The first station to be provided with a stock of women was established in Manchukuo itself between 1932 and 1933. By the start of 1938 between 30,000 and 40,000 sex slaves, primarily Korean, had already been processed into this abysmal system. In 1993 Japanese Chief Cabinet Secretary Yohei Kono acknowledged the terrible injustices faced by these women, whom the Japanese had euphemistically called 'comfort Women'.[5] These memories are still very much alive in both Koreas and are well incorporated into North Korea's propaganda.

From Confucius to Kim Il-sung

When he joined the anti-Japanese resistance, Kim Song-ju took the nom de guerre of Kim Il-sung. He had the perfect pedigree for the resistance fighter. His father had been involved in subversive activities against the Japanese empire; in 1935 his middle brother had been arrested in Manchukuo and died while in the hands of the Japanese; and his mother's brother spent thirteen years in a Japanese prison. With this background it is easy to interweave tales of the years he spent as a guerrilla fighter with legends that depict him as a Far Eastern Robin Hood, the man who brought deliverance to the Koreans.[6]

In one of these heroic stories, Kim Il-sung steals from the aristocracy in Kapsan, across the border from

Manchuria, to feed his guerrilla fighters. Kapsan, at the foot of the White Head Mountains, was one of the poorest regions of Korea and a stronghold of the Korean aristocracy. Peasants had gone hungry for centuries and often described their condition as a perennial stream of hunger, admitting to eating tree bark and wild roots to fend off starvation.

From Manchuria, where he initially established his headquarters, Kim Il-sung led his guerrillas to take back the land from the Korean landlords and the Japanese colonisers and handed it over to the peasants. The agrarian system he applied was similar to the Soviet model introduced in the USSR. Well before the birth of the new nation, in this region Kim established collectivisation and agrarian base camps. This process, which de facto dismantled for the first time the ancient Korean feudal system, was a successful experiment that in the 1950s greatly influenced the future agrarian reform in North Korea.

Even more symbolic for the nation-building narrative of North Korea is another story, which recounts the liberation of a group of victims of both the Chinese communists and the Japanese colonisers in Manchuria. This tale sets the stage for Kim's unique vision of society and ideology, *juche*, which, as we shall see, North Koreans regard as a step forward from communism.

One bitter winter day in 1935, Kim Il-sung and his guerrilla fighters arrived at a locked log cabin on Mount Ma'an, near present-day Ciqikou, on the west bank of the Jialing river in central Manchuria. When they opened the door, they found dozens of people clothed in rags, starving, sick and scared. The fighters soon learned who they were: the surviving victims of a pogrom that Chinese communists and Japanese colonisers had conducted in the area. Kim freed them and welcomed them into his guerrilla group.

Among them were twenty to thirty children, orphans of members of the resistance or of the victims of the purges the counter-insurgency was constantly carrying out. The woman who looked after these children, named Kim Chong-suk, was so petite she could be easily mistaken for one of the children herself. Kim would eventually marry her and together they would become the parents of all the orphans of the resistance and of the Korean War. As a couple they would go on to establish the nation of North Korea, the Democratic People's Republic of Korea (DPRK), extending their parental role to all its inhabitants and shaping the newly born country as a family-nation. Eventually, the *juche* doctrine would legitimise this peculiar presentation of Kim Il-sung as the wise leader, the father and protector of the community, and Kim Chong-suk as his beloved wife and partner, the mother of the nation and its future rulers.

The first brick of the parental nation-building project came from the orphans of the independence and, later, at the beginning of the 1950s, from the orphans of the Korean War. They represented the critical mass of the new nation's future generations, hence the attention that even today the North Korean leadership pays to orphans. In 1947 Kim established a boarding school for these children, the School for the Offspring of Revolutionary Martyrs. Later renamed Man'gyongdae Revolutionary School, it became the incubator of the future top-ranking members of the DPRK. Kim Jong-il, the son of Kim Il-sung and Kim Chong-suk, also attended the school. In the 1960s, when *juche* became the state doctrine, the orphans participated in rewriting the narrative of the war of independence. One of their key contributions was to change the birthplace of Kim Jong-il, who was born in a Soviet camp in Kabarovsk in 1942, to the sacred Mount Paektu, in the north of the country.[7] Mount Paektu became an important symbol of the *juche* mythology. Thus, the orphans were elected custodians and interpreters of the soul of the new nation, a country and a people that their adoptive parents had shaped for them.

To understand the concept of a family-nation, it is imperative to analyse the role that Confucius (551–479 BC) still plays in Korean culture. At the centre of both Korean and Chinese society, one finds the family, the nucleus of Confucian ethics. Confucius traces the architecture of society back to five relationships: ruler to subject, father to son, elder brother to younger brother, husband to wife, and friend to friend. Apart from the first and last, all are blood ties. The relationships are never equal, not even those between friends, but are based on precise, well-codified social values and norms and on the Confucian ideal of *ren*. This concept defines the individual. A good way to explain *ren* is to use the corresponding Chinese ideogram, which is composed of two parts: a man standing next to the number two, which signifies plurality. Hence the individual exists only in relation to the other; plurality and not individualism describes humanity. Thus, for the Chinese and the Koreans the individual does not count by themself, but only in relation to others.

Inside the family, ancestor veneration stresses the importance of family cohesion.[8] In politics, the ideal ruler is 'like the polar star, which by keeping its place makes all the other stars revolve round it'. With this maxim, Confucius intended to emphasise the importance of the ruler as an example for their subjects to follow, regardless of the rigidity of the laws. This is as if to say, if the sovereign is good and virtuous, so his subjects will be, and the society will be harmonious.[9] It follows that unity and stability depend on hierarchy. Individual, family and state are regulated by an ethical code valid at all levels: in the family, children respect their parents; in society, the young honour the old; and in the state, submission of administrator to ruler prevails. Unlike in Hobbes's *Leviathan*, in this vision human nature remains essentially positive. With the right schooling and family guidance, the individual may assimilate a system of values and ethical behaviour that permits him to interact properly in society. At the same time, anyone can rise to the top of the social scale on his own merits.

At the core of North Korean society one finds, rather than pure Marxism, a reinterpretation of *ren* where 'the father' takes on a new meaning, namely 'the supreme leader', the founding father of the nation. At the same time the dynastic tradition of ancient Korea is maintained, where the supreme leader's family is at the core of the family-nation, whose role is to protect the extended family of citizens, hence the hereditary nature of the North Korean political system. In the Constitution of 1972, the family nucleus is identified as a cell in the body of society and the state as an organism looking after its cells. Kim Il-sung, Kim Jong-il and today Kim Jong-un are the custodians of this body-state and their task is to make sure it performs as expected. 'The masses who are not led by a wise leader can be likened to a body without a brain', wrote Kim Jong-il.[10]

Although in North Korea Marxism proved handy in dismantling the feudal system, becoming the blueprint for the agrarian reform, it was not used in the nation-building process of the DPRK as it had been in Russia or China.

The Bond of Hunger

The mythologies of Mao and Kim are often set against the backdrop of a land of starving peasants. The populations of China and Korea, as the victims of brutal colonisers engaged in a global war, could barely feed themselves. From this bleak setting, the two men emerged as the leaders of armies in rags with one constant companion: hunger.

It is difficult for Westerners to understand the relationship between hunger and politics in modern times. True, the French revolution showed us that people take to the streets and stage revolutions when they go hungry, but decades and decades of hunger, in a colonised country devastated by a foreign occupier in the nineteenth and twentieth centuries, is somehow different from the rioting of Parisians in 1789. Lack of infrastructure coupled with deep poverty turned hunger into a permanent nightmare for the deeply proud nations of China and Korea. Year after year, this hunger stripped men and women of their traditions and of their humanity, forcing them to revert to their basic animal instincts. It is in this context that one has to analyse the atrocities committed in China, in Manchuria and in Korea in the 1930s and the 1940s.

As the mythology goes, Mao and Kim maintained and expressed their human qualities against all odds. Many of the legends about Kim Il-sung are fairytales of a man who is able to bring his starving guerrillas back from the brink of dehumanisation, a man battling constantly against injustice, not simply over the lack of food, but also the lack of freedom. Later on, after the birth of the Democratic People's Republic of Korea, these stories kept alive the memories of the years of hunger for those who had survived those horrific times. They became part of the narrative of the strong father-leader who saved the family-nation not only from the brutal Japanese regime but from dehumanisation. The bond of hunger between Kim and the North Korean people became a strong, unshakable connection, so solid that, as we shall see, in the 1990s, after his death, it withstood another tragic bout of hunger.

The Purest Race

The Korea that emerged from the first half of the twentieth century was deeply traumatised. One could argue that those years had a similar impact on most of the world and that from the ashes of two world wars rose a new world order where the contemporary, deeply traumatised nation-states took their first steps. Nationalism and racism, common features of the decades leading up to World War II, were rejected as nation-building tools and instead recognised as the root causes of the global conflict.

Not in Korea!

Korean society internalised the concept of racial superiority that the Japanese had preached, and repackaged it as the primary engine of the anti-colonial struggle and of its victory over a foreign power. It was embraced as the essence of the national identity of the modern Korea. Both Koreas identify their legitimacy in the exceptional racial traits of the Korean race, as witnessed in the victorious struggle against the Japanese oppressor.

In the 1960s, South Korean President Park Chung-hee promoted the ideology of racial purity to legitimise his authoritarian rule in South Korea. Even today, those living on both sides of the thirty-eighth parallel believe that they belong to the purest race. A racial divide in South Korea has recently flared up again in relation to foreign migrants, people who in the last decades have moved from other Asian countries, attracted by the Korean economic boom. Koreans look down on them and young people express the same racial prejudice of their parents and grandparents vis-à-vis foreigners.[11]

For now let us focus on how the North and South Korean national identity was shaped around the racial superiority concept. No country emerges from colonisation without scars. In 1905, when Japan established a protectorate in Korea, Japan promoted the idea that the two nations had the same racial stock; essentially they shared a bloodline. The core of this racial theory was the notion of *minjok,* defined as a group of people with common ancestry who reside in the same area, have the same history, share a common religion and use the same language. The forced Japanisation of Korea and the attempts to eradicate Korea's culture were aimed at proving these theories. After the capitulation of Japan, Korean scholars and intellectuals redefined the concept of *minjok* to describe a warlike race that had fought bravely to preserve Korean identity, a pure race that had declined and had been reinvigorated by anti-colonisation sentiment.

Erasing the pro-Japanese role that the Korean aristocracy had played during the years of occupation, especially in the south, a new narrative emerged whereby colonisation had produced a resurgence of a dormant, yet exceptional, racial strength.[12] When the north and the south were fighting to shape a new nation, in the aftermath of World War II as well as during the Korean War, both Koreas shared the racial belief of the uniqueness of the Korean *minjok.* For both regimes, armies and people, it was and still is the primary explanation of the resistance and victory over the Japanese empire which led to the birth of their nations.

Kim Il-sung understood the appeal of the racial doctrine for the collective imagination of his followers. He also realised it could become a useful instrument to curb some of the negative traits he had witnessed among the Korean diaspora, such as disunity. Kim had fought a long guerrilla war with an army of people from all walks of life: along with the peasants and the labourers there were the communists, the nationalists, the bandits and the criminals. He had witnessed merchants, Japanese collaborators and businessmen all pledging their loyalties to whoever was in power at that moment, and he judged these characteristics as a poor foundation for a long-lasting nation. He promised himself that the new state would be created under the banner of unity, no matter what that implied. The idea of racial superiority came very handy. He promoted a society that did not tolerate any form of dissent or political alternative, that was racially so pure and so superior that it had to be totally self-sufficient.[13] A self-reliant nation did not need the outside world. The motto was: one country, one nation, one ethnicity, one collective political thought.

The first test came in 1950 with the outbreak of the Korean War.

Facts and Fiction about the Korean War

Korea has been described by the Japanese as 'a dagger pointed at the heart of Japan' and by the Chinese as 'a hammer ready to strike at the head of China'. Over the centuries, bigger players in the region have watched Korea closely and often decisions taken outside its borders, rather than inside, have shaped its destiny. Yet neither the long centuries of domination by imperial China, when Korea was a tributary state, nor the annexation to imperial Japan in 1910, have erased the strong sense of identity of the Korean people. Not even the division between north and south and the civil war have altered the fundamental feeling that Korea is one country and Koreans are one race.[14] It is against this extraordinary background that one has to analyse the Korean War (1950–53), a fratricidal and deeply traumatic conflict for the people of the Korean peninsula.

When a colonial empire collapses under the hammer of a victorious enemy, its colonies become the spoils of war. Borders are moved and new countries pop up at the stroke of a pen. At the end of World War II, the conflicting influences of the two superpowers, USA and Russia, required the breakup of the Korean peninsula, a dramatic decision that eventually produced the first conflict of the Cold War.

As early as 1945, the Americans, who also had occupied Japan, marched into South Korea, while the Russians moved to the North. The common narrative is that the USSR backed Kim Il-sung in the North, that he was a puppet in the hands of Stalin and that he managed to grab power in 1948 only thanks to Moscow. According to this interpretation, the Soviets had a well-developed plan for North Korea, which featured Kim Il-sung as its leader. This reconstruction of events could not be further from the truth. Stalin never trusted the Korean communists – indeed, in the 1930s he gave the order to shoot all Korean agents in the Comintern, with the excuse that they could be Japanese collaborators.[15] He used the same justification to deport 200,000 Koreans, many of whom were immigrants, from the Soviet Far East to central Asia, primarily to Kazakhstan and Uzbekistan. Stalin did not particularly like Kim Il-sung either and until 1946, Moscow was considering backing the nationalist leader Cho Man-sik.[16] Like Mao, Kim had conducted a revolution with an army of peasants who literally venerated him, and Stalin disliked this type of hero because they might cast a shadow over his own role as supreme leader of the communist universe.

More likely, Kim Il-sung managed to get hold of power in North Korea for a simple reason: in the aftermath of World War II, the Russians were too busy carving up the Eastern European bloc and paid little attention to Korea. Kim was quick to seize this oppor-tunity. He was smart.

South of the thirty-eighth parallel, the Americans showed a similar lack of focus and understanding as their former allies, the Russians, had demonstrated in the north of the peninsula. They placed in charge of South Korea an exiled politician who had spent thirteen years in the Uniteed States, Syngman Rhee, and who openly declared that his aim was to impose national unity by force. He had no local connections, no understanding of the situation on the ground and no political finesse.

Against this background, what chance did Korea have to be reunified peacefully? Well beyond the dispute about the casus belli of the war – which army crossed the thirty-eighth parallel first, the one from the North or the one from the South? – the root cause of the Korean War rests with the geopolitical position of the peninsula. Instead of promoting reconciliation, Moscow and Washington began challenging each other from opposite sides of the thirty-eighth parallel, a game of cat and mouse they would go on playing in the following decades at a global level, inside nations that happened to be located along the geopolitical boundaries of their spheres of influence. Sometimes Moscow or Washington would use their own military power, as in Vietnam or Korea; other times they would fight via substitutes, armed groups they sponsored, as in the case of the proxy wars in Central America.

One thing is sure, in 1945 neither of the two superpowers wanted an independent and unified Korea. They were both anxious that such a nation would not fall into the other's sphere of influence, and so Korea was divided and remained divided. The Russians did not want an American 'protectorate' on their border and the Americans certainly feared the birth of a Soviet satellite state in the Far East, as confirmed by their engagement in the Vietnam War. Ironically, had that happened, most likely the North Korean regime would not have lasted so long. With the implosion of the Soviet Union, Korea would have shared the same destiny as Eastern Europe. Once again, the geopolitical position of Korea sealed its political destiny, making it easy prey for foreign powers.

The Koreans bear some of the responsibility for this outcome. On opposite sides of the thirty-eighth parallel, people were not ready to put an end to the hostility that had characterised the previous three decades, a resentment that, it became clear after 1945, was fuelled by the ideology of patriotism. Both the North and the South claimed to have fought a war of independence against the Japanese and demanded the right to be considered the sole true Korean patriots. To prove this, they accused each other of treason. The South saw Kim Il-sung and his guerrillas as Soviet cronies, while the North dismissed the South as Japanese collaborators and, after 1945, American lackeys. The patriotic dispute crystallised during World War II and, by the time the conflict ended, was so internalised among people at the top of the ruling pyramids of both Koreas that all they wanted was to wipe out the internal enemy and reunify the country under their banner.[17] Of course, the Soviets and the Americans did not understand the nature of the clash between the two Koreas, so they did not predict the outbreak of the war.

The Korean War, the first war-by-proxy of the Cold War, soon became a textbook case of what superpowers should *not* do when engaged in nation building; mistakes that the last one still standing, the United States, keeps repeating even today, for example in the Middle East.[18] From 1945 to 1948, during the US occupation of Korea, the Americans empowered an entire generation of Koreans who had served Japanese imperialism and fought against the Allies during World War II. They were so focused on the new enemy, the USSR, that they forgot about the old one. The USA put them in charge of the military and of the national police, regardless of the role they had played before. In the summer of 1949, the South Korean commander of the thirty-eighth parallel was Kim Sok-won, who had been a Japanese collaborator in the 1930s and had pursued Kim Il-sung and other guerrillas in Manchuria while working for the Japanese Kwantung Army.[19] But Korean people had a better memory and resented these decisions. Does this sound familiar? Just look at Iraq and Syria today: in the former regions of the Caliphate, the Sunni population is once again discriminated against by the Shia, the Kurds, the Iraqis and even the Assad regime.[20] The Korean War was the rehearsal for the fiascos of the future.

The Korean War also helps us understand the delicate relationship between North Korea and China, the new superpower. When the Americans drove the North Koreans to the northern border, near the Yalu river, which separates China from the DPRK, Chinese soldiers, mostly volunteers, were dispatched to help Kim Il-sung's troops. A Chinese war veteran remembers that at a certain stage Kim Il-sung crossed over to China and remained under the protection of Mao's army. According to his account, China's intervention saved the North from capitulating. Chinese troops crossed the border and fought US troops to avoid having a pro-Washington regime on their border.[21] Mao did not let Kim Il-sung's regime collapse because the DPRK was born as a buffer state to protect China from the United States. For seventy years it has performed this task very well and there is no reason why it should stop doing so today.

The ideology that sold the Korean War to the Americans and to the world ignores these facts and centres on the dichotomy between good and evil; it is identical to the one used today to justify the conflict in the Middle East. A simplistic lie manufactured to hide the complexity of modern geopolitics. By 1950, when the Korean War began, America was consumed by anti-communist fever. Senator McCarthy had ignited a fire in Washington that was burning across the entire continent. Communism was perceived as the ultimate evil because it was depicted as being essentially inhuman,[22] hence, the massive, disproportionate military reaction to the red flags of Kim Il-sung's army crossing the thirty-eighth parallel.

The evil nature of the enemy handily justified, in public opinion, a bombing campaign that brought unimaginable destruction to the North, far beyond what had happened in Germany or Japan. The United States dropped 635,000 tons of bombs in Korea and 32,557 tons of napalm, compared to 503,000 tons of bombs in the entire Pacific during World War II. 'The Americans bombed North Korea so much that there were no more targets to bomb', said General In-Bum Chun, top ranking officer in South Korea, in the BBC documentary *North Korea's Nuclear Trump Card*.[23] 'The North Koreans still remember the bombing.' Of the twenty-two major cities, eighteen were obliterated by half.[24] Even by World War II standards, the Korean War was atrocious. Anthony Herbert, who fought in the war, writes in his book *Soldier* that just a year into the conflict, General MacArthur admitted to the US Congress that he had never seen such devastation.[25] Curtis LeMay, who took over from MacArthur, later wrote, 'We burned down just about every city in North Korea and South Korea both...we killed off over a million civilian Koreans and drove several million more from their homes.'[26] Was such massive military destruction predominantly a warning to Moscow and Beijing?

When in 1953 a truce was reached, it is estimated that around 2.5 million civilians had either been wounded, killed, abducted or had gone missing.[27] China and the USSR, for sure, received the message and even today they have not forgotten it. North Korea became an important, strategic buffer between two worlds.

The Koreans also have not forgotten the message. The lack of a peace treaty made reconciliation impossible, freezing into place over time an animosity between the North and the South that would not thaw. Today, Koreans still point fingers across the thirty-eighth parallel, accusing each other of treason.

Juche: The Scientology of Totalitarianism

The Korean War also sent a clear message to Kim Il-sung. It became apparent that North Korea was geographically sandwiched between communism and capitalism and that was not a good position to be in; to make sure the country would never again experience such destruction, implementing self-reliance was imperative as much as building a powerful military machine. Kim Il-sung began working at a way to isolate and insulate the country from those powers, and so produced a new doctrine: *juche*.

The first thing that strikes anybody who attempts to understand *juche* is its lack of clarity. Kim was a brilliant guerrilla fighter but he was not an ideologue. He struggled to flesh out a comprehensive theory. *Juche* is a poor ideology, full of unconnected principles, absurd concepts and even contradictory slogans. How do you reconcile one of its fundamental tenets, that man is the master of all things and decides everything, with another, that the state, its leaders and its political vision come before the interests and identities of individuals? It is only when analysed as a modern religion, similar to Scientology, a non–transcendental doctrine with a twist of absurdity and plenty of dogmas, that *juche* begins to make sense.

A European diplomat I interviewed who has spent several years in Pyongyang agrees that, as a nation, North Korea presents a strong religious component, which makes it impossible to analyse it rationally.

North Korea is a mystery even for people like me, who have lived in Pyongyang for four years. It is still impossible to present a rational explanation of how this country and its people function...While I was living in North Korea, I met a lot of journalists and read their articles, I have always come to the same conclusion: what they have written does not make any sense. They all try to find a rational key to describe North Korea to their reader but none works.

At the core of *juche* is a well-crafted story of creation. In the beginning there was the purest race, the Koreans. They lived in the best land on earth and had no desire to go anywhere else. They did not know that the outside world was envious, that it wanted to grab their beautiful land and enslave them. So when the Japanese army invaded the peninsula, Koreans were stunned and did not know what to do, hence they ended up being colonised. At that time, they were not conscious of their own strength and uniqueness. The awakening came with the arrival of a truly exceptional hero, Kim Il-sung. He freed the people from the chains of Japanese colonisation, offered them deliverance and eternal physical protection from the menace of the outside world, and gave them *juche,* a code of behaviour that guarantees the darkness of the past will never come back.

In a nutshell this is what the North Korean masses religiously believe: that, although they are an ancient people and have always been racially superior to everybody else, they became a true nation only seventy years ago, when Kim Il-sung shaped the new state. 'Before liberation our country was under Japanese rule for about forty years. Before liberation the grandparents lived in harsh poverty. Kim Il-sung led a twenty-year long arduous, anti-Japanese armed struggle. And finally liberated our country.' This is how a North Korean woman summarises the parable of the creation of her country.[28]

As it is with Christianity or Islam, a big component of the *juche* creed is revelation. 'The leader discovered the truth of the *juche* idea in the course of the struggle against bigoted nationalists and bogus Marxists, flunkeyism and dogmatists, while hewing out a new path for revolution', wrote Kim Jong-il in *The Juche Philosophy*, a book in which he spelled out the meaning of *juche*.[29] In the ultimate analysis, Kim Il-sung is the *juche* messiah and his holiness can be transmitted to his offspring, as reported by Evan Osnos in *The New Yorker*. This is what he wrote about a visit to a school for orphans:

I stood in front of a large photo of Kim (Kim Jong-un) touching a fuzzy red blanket. The principal stepped aside, and, with a flourish, revealed, in a Plexiglas box, the blanket. 'He personally touched it,' he said. So it was with other specimens – the white painted chair that he blessed with his presence in the lunchroom; the simple wooden chair from the language lab, on which he rested from his labours – all preserved under glass, like the relics of a saint. I asked Pak Yong Chul how it felt to be visited by the leader, and his eyes widened. 'That moment is unforgettable. I would never have dreamed of it,' he said.[30]

Revelation happened while Kim the messiah was fighting the enemy, during a vicious war against the Japanese army. It was not a magic, mythical moment, as when Emperor Constantine had a vision and saw over the Roman bridge that separated him from his enemies a splendid cross with the writing 'under this banner you shall win', but a process that took place over several years. As with all religions, the *juche* narrative incorporates superstitions and mythological stories, most of which are old Korean tales repackaged to fit the story of Kim's revelation and creation.

In the Bible, God created the world in seven days from the sky; in *The Juche Philosophy*, Kim Il-sung created North Korea during the war of independence from his headquarters in Mount Paektu, at the border between China and North Korea. Mount Paektu is the highest mountain in North Korea and in northern China and is an active volcano. It is also a sacred place for people living on both sides of the thirty-eighth parallel because, according to Korean mythology, it was the birthplace of Tangun, the founder of the first Korean kingdom, Gojoseon (2333–108 BC).[31] 'The founding father of our nation was Tangun', writes Kim Jong-il, 'and the founding father of socialist Korea was the great leader Comrade Kim Il-sung'.[32] The mountain's mythology plays an important role in the legitimation of the *juche* ideology as well as of North Korea because it links the present to the beginning of time for the Korean nation. This explains why it is often used in North Korea's propaganda, for example, the Paektu rocket and its peak feature in the North Korean emblem. Article 169 of the Constitution describes it as 'the sacred mountain of the revolution'.[33] It is now clear why the orphans of the war of independence suggested to Kim Il-sung Mount Paektu as the birthplace of Kim Jong-il.

Unlike the revelations of Christianity and Islam, the *juche* revelation was not immediately publicised – the first time Kim Il-sung mentioned it was in 1955. *Juche* was not presented as a religious creed but as an ideology similar to communism, an improvement of communism. Like Scientology, which was not constructed as a religion but as a philosophy and ideology, *juche* was born in the 1950s, in the post-World War II traumatised landscape, a period in which many philosophical theories about the origins and meaning of humankind blossomed. Also like Scientology, *juche* evolved into the faith of a sect – the North Koreans – when it became clear that this was the only avenue for the country's long-term survival. Both Scientology and *juche* reset the clock of history according to revelation and, by doing so, drew a line under the traumatic past. The North Korean calendar, the *juche* calendar, starts with the birth of Kim Il-sung in 1912, while Scientology uses the AD abbreviation not for anno Domini, but 'After Dianetics', the first brick of L. Ron Hubbard's new world.[34]

The need to produce a new ideology most likely became a priority in 1953 when Stalin died. His death led to an internal fight for succession and to the outbreak of Moscow and Beijing's antagonism. Kim understood the urgency to produce *juche* to keep and maintain a distance from North Korea's two big communist neighbours, to avoid being gobbled up by one of them. Hence, at the core of *juche* is the concept of self-reliance. By shutting off the world, North Korea was going to avoid once more being the prey of foreign powers and falling victim to a foreign ideology or being flattened once again by foreign military aviation. The key words of *juche* are *chaju,* which means political and ideological independence, especially from the Soviet Union and China; *charip,* which is economic self-reliance and self-sufficiency; and *chawi,* military independence and a viable national defence system.[35] As we shall see, acquiring nuclear capability became paramount to fulfilling the latter.

Producing the new ideology took quite some time and could not have been easy. In fact it was only in 1972 that *juche* was crowned North Korea's national ideology. The North Korean Constitution stipulates in Article 3 that the North Korean government 'shall make the *Juche* Ideology of the Workers' Party the guiding principle for all its actions' and the Workers' Party Charter states in a preamble that, 'the Workers' Party is guided only by Kim Il-sung's *Juche* Ideology and revolutionary thoughts'.[36] Over the twenty years of its formation, *juche* emerged from the progressive stripping of the tenets of Soviet and Chinese communism and their replacement with elements of Korean ethnocentric nationalism and of Japanese racial theories. These were principles people could easily relate to because, like the concept of the purity of the Korean race, they had been ingrained in Korean culture during millennia of dynastic rule. *Juche* incorporated these elements of ancient mythology, superstition and racial theory and morphed them into North Korea's modern nationalism.

In Italy, Mussolini created fascism from Italian parochialism, superstition and ancient legends through a similar ideological cleanse. But while Il Duce, as Mussolini was known, was able only to manufacture a successful cult of personality, Kim Il-sung achieved much more: he established in the twentieth century a blood dynasty and a religion.

It's like a religion. From birth, you learn about the Kim family, learn that they are gods, that you must be absolutely obedient to the Kim family. The elites are treated nicely, and because of that they make sure that the system stays stable.[37]

In the aftermath of World War II and of a brutal colonisation, Koreans responded positively to *juche*. They had no problem believing in the exceptional, supernatural qualities of Kim and of his bloodline. Even today, North Koreans often use the expression *Paektu hyultong* or 'Paektu bloodline' to describe Kim Jong-un's legitimacy as their leader. 'Korea will always emerge victorious in the future under the wise leadership of the respected comrade Kim Jong-un, who was born to continue the line of "Mangyongade" revolutionary family', explains a North Korean woman.[38] We must remember that both the Confucian Korean dynastic monarchies and the Japanese empire were built on the assumption that the purity of the bloodline dictates who will rise and who will fall. Historically and culturally, therefore, Koreans had never experienced anything different!

After 1972, the *juche* doctrine continued to be perfected to fit the needs of the new dynasty and to shape its bond with the new nation. In 1980 Kim Il-sung introduced the theory of the Immortal Socio-Political Body, which was incorporated into the *juche* doctrine and can be summarised as follows: the *suryong* (leader) is an impeccable brain of the living body, the masses can be endowed with their life in exchange for their loyalty to him, and the party is the nervous system of that living body. In other words, without the *suryong,* which is the brain, and the party, which is the nervous system, the masses will remain dead limbs because they are no more than arms and legs.[39]

In this scenario, God and communism become irrelevant; indeed, the transcendental God historically never existed in the North Korean mind while communism was instrumental only to the discovery of *juche.* At the core of the new religion is Kim Il-sung, a man with supernatural powers who is at the same time the creator of North Korea and the nation itself. As in the Christian trinity, Kim is one man and every North Korean man, woman and child at the same time. A people drenched in Confucianism who had in the past brushed shoulders with Buddhism had no problem accepting the first *juche* dogma.

Then there is the holiness of Kim's bloodline, strong enough to be able to protect the nation and to prevent the outside world from enslaving its people again. The question of succession, as in any communist country, has never arisen in North Korea. The bloodline establishes the succession from Kim Il-sung to his son Kim Jong-il.[40] The only choice in the succession was which son was better suited to step into the shoes of the father, to act as the messenger of the eternal leader. The vicarious role of Kim Jong-il and of Kim Jong-un today sprang from yet another *juche* dogma: Kim Il-sung died but he will always be the eternal leader of North Korea, he lives on inside the body of the community.

'For the everybody, no matter how educated they are, the regime is like a religion', explains the European diplomat who spent four years in Pyongyang.

> I asked someone I knew well and with whom I sometime could have a profound discussion, I asked him if all those people that stand in line in front of the monument of the leader on those special day, if they truly believe that he is the eternal leader. He said, well, maybe five in one hundred not, but the rest yes. This is basically everybody. For me in four years the real hardship [of an expat's life in the DPRK] has been the absolute lack of loyalty towards me and us as an institution, the people remain one hundred per cent religiously loyal to the regime, and this is the tough life for us foreigners.

A corollary of the dogma of the eternal leader refers to the immortality of North Koreans. *Juche* describes human beings as members of a socio-political community that is a living body, hence there is no individual apart from the community. As the community survives, there will be some sort of continued existence, a form of immortality for members of the community even when their bodies die.

Whatever one thinks of North Korea, it is remarkable and at the same time shocking that *juche*, a racial and nationalistic creed, was developed in the second half of the twentieth century, when racial theories were shunned elsewhere. In North Korea, on the contrary, the purity of the bloodline became a discriminating factor that inevitably led to the formation of a caste system, the *songbun,* and to the isolation of the nation to avoid contamination from the rest of the world. Even today, North Koreans are ranked according to family history; those whose grandparents fought with Kim Il-sung as well as the orphans are considered to have the purest blood. But loyalty to the government, that is, to the leadership, also plays a big role.

Parents are required to register the birth of a baby, with information about the new citizen kept in three places: at the local town hall, with the police and with the secret police. The first thing a new-born gets from the state is its *songbun* – one of the five social statuses allocated to all North Koreans. Depending on the status of the father, the infant will be classified as either 'special', 'nucleus', 'basic', 'complex' or 'hostile'. A policeman will stamp the *songbun* on the baby's new file, establishing where this North Korean will be allowed to live, which university it will be able to enter, where it might work and whether it will be able to join the Korean Workers' party.[41]

In the lowest classes are those with family roots in South Korea and Japan, which, together with the United States, are North Korea's biggest enemies. Robert Collins, who has worked in South Korea for three decades for the Department of Defence, in his study of *songbun*, reported the following story: Mr Hong-il graduated from high school and was drafted into the air force. He did so well that his superior recommended him for entrance into Kim Il-sung Political College. However, it emerged that during the Korean War his father defected to the North from the South. Hence his *songbun* was not good to attend such a high-level college. He ended up being sent to work in the mines as a labourer.[42]

As in Scientology, the members of the *juche* community are considered exceptional and not everybody can join in. Building on the historical ethno-nationalism of Korea, *juche* sanctions the superiority of North Koreans over their brothers and sisters in South Korea who have not embraced the *juche* revelation and have been contaminated by the Americans.[43] Ultimately, the *juche* creed legitimises the existence of North Korea by instilling in its people the purest kind of ethnic pride. And this explains why not many people are leaving the country: not because someone is guarding the borders, but because they cannot imagine living outside such borders.[44]

Even those who have moved out of North Korea look at *juche* with a mix of pride and nostalgia, as emerged from several interviews with North Koreans who have left the country. Research based on 100 structured interviews with North Korean citizens legally residing in China shows that nearly two-thirds of the respondents 'indicate that they are either "exceedingly proud" or "moderately proud" of the *Juche* idea'.[45] The vast majority also supports unification for the purpose of promoting economic development in North Korea. North Koreans are not interested in the disappearance of their regime but in economic improvement. The respect for *juche* confirms that, for the North Korean, the legitimacy of the state rests on this religious/ideological construction more than on the collective memory of what North Korea once was, that is, part of the Korean kingdom.

Juche has been instrumental in maintaining a distinct sense of North Korean-ness, originally created by and continually reproduced through North Korea's state-nationalism. This religious glue has kept the nation united even when facing the frequent failures of the state to provide basic public goods. In a nutshell, this is the uniqueness of North Korean national identity, different from that of their relatives in the South.

Chapter 2

Broken Identity

Both North and South Koreans used the purity of their race as the foundation and legitimacy for their nation. Such a tool can be very tricky, however. For a start, a racially homogeneous and pure state requires a firm stand on the rest of the world; all the others, those ethnically different, end up representing the boundaries that should never be crossed. Naturally, the geography of the 'outside world' appears different if looked at from the northern or southern side of the thirty-eighth parallel. Kim Il-sung's Korea was suspicious of everybody, including communist Russia and China; the South Korean leadership was less selective and, at least initially, embraced the United States.[1] In a fashion well tested during the Cold War, the distinct and divergent visions of foreign lands, cultures and nations became propaganda food for Koreans.

It may sound surreal, but the Korean peninsula is still inhabited by the ghost of the Cold War. Indeed, the two nations were shaped in the battlefield where the mighty United States and the big Soviet Russia first confronted each other. Other nations suffered a similar fate and were able to reunify. But not Korea. The contemporary history of this peninsula is still the tale of sharply different visions of the world, divergent commercial and economic interests, and a conflict among strong men, dictators and generals. The world knows very little about it. Drenched in propaganda and recycled history, focusing on keeping the world at arm's length to protect their racial purity, neither state has been forthcoming in exposing its recent history, preferring to remain prisoner of an ideological dichotomy that today appears totally anachronistic.

In 1948, while the North took the road of communism and, later, of *juche*, the South remained under the wing of Western capitalism and authoritarianism for several decades and eventually joined the Asian Tigers, linking its legitimacy to anti-communist nationalism first and economic growth soon after. Until the 1980s, South Korea was ruled by repressive government and dictatorship. During those decades, freedom of speech was not allowed and political repression, assassinations and torture were not uncommon. While the world recovered from World War II and enjoyed the economic boom of the 1960s, Koreans on both sides of the thirty-eighth parallel continued to suffer and struggled to come to terms with a mutilation that split the core of their society: the family.

An interesting question is why reunification in Korea has not taken place. The desire for reunification has historically been very popular among the people of both the North and South.[2] The answer does not rest on the Demilitarised Zone – the iron curtain was equally daunting; nor on the totalitarianism of North Korea and the authoritarianism of South Korea – people have successfully objected similar regimes; nor on the resilience of the North Korean regime – there have been several opportunities for a collapse. The answer rests in the ability of the founding fathers of the modern Korean nations to manipulate Korean ethnicity in order to mobilise their populations in opposition to the 'other' Korea. This has been possible because the Korean ethnicity/race has long been indistinguishable from the Korean nation. In other words, the justification of each Korea is the negation of the right of the other to exist.

As early as 1948, clinging to their strong sense of pride, those living in the North and those in the South began competing with each other, not only to claim the crown of true patriots of the Korean people, but to justify the breakup of their own country. Both sides wanted to prove that their Korea was the real one while the other was an aberration. As the two nations had embraced two distinct economic and political models, communism and capitalism, the confrontation perfectly slotted into the Cold War ideological dichotomy.

A Tale of Two Nationalisms

At the end of World War II, the same patriotism and ethno-nationalism became the magic wand of nation building in the South as well as in the North. Though both countries were occupied by foreign powers, North and South Koreans believed that it was their own heroism, not the outcome of World War II, that had kicked the Japanese out. While in the North the proof of such a vision came from the warrior/Robin Hood mythology constructed around Kim Il-sung, in the South other heroes of the anti-colonial struggle were used to cement this belief. Many of the southern heroes were also celebrated in the North, though their status never got close to Kim Il-sung or to his bloodline. Among them was Ahn Jung-geun.[3]

Ahn Jung-geun was an independence fighter who, on 26 October 1909, on the verge of the annexation of Korea to Japan, assassinated Ito Hirobumi, a four-time prime minister of Japan and the first governor-general of Korea. He was tried and executed soon after. In North Korea, school children study his life as one of the true Korean patriots. However, it is in the South that Ahn is celebrated as the most important national hero of independence, to the extent that his life has been instrumental to the shaping of the South Korean national identity.

It is apparent that Kim Il-sung's decades-long battle against the Japanese and Ahn Jung-geun's heroic gesture cannot be compared. They were both heroes of the anti-Japanese resistance, though the latter was executed while still in his late twenties. The anti-colonial fight had been concentrated in the north and in Manchuria, so it's to be expected that the South does not have strong, legendary figures like Kim Il-sung. To construct the national identity of South Korea upon the anti-Japanese resistance, another powerful heroic emblem was needed, someone who could compete with Kim Il-sung. Without it South Korea could not have claimed to be the rightful heir of a thousand-year national history and the guardian of the 'spirit' of the anti-Japanese resistance. Anti-communist nationalism seemed to be perfect for this task. Hence, as Japan capitulated, South Korean propaganda began accusing Kim Il-sung of being a traitor, to have handed over half the nation to the Soviets.

History was quickly recycled. Pyongyang became Seoul's enemy. The Democratic People's Republic of Korea, whose nationalism was inextricably linked to Kim Il-sung and the revolutionary, anti-Japanese heritage of his guerrilla warfare, became the benchmark of deceit. Interestingly, the United States and the Soviet Union, which had been allies during World War II, soon got engaged in a similar rewriting of their past. The outbreak of the Korean War in 1950 sealed this new reading of history, which held until the fall of the Berlin Wall in 1989. One could say that the seeds of inevitability of the Cold War were sown in Korea.

Once history had been rewritten, competition between the two Koreas, as between the USA and the USSR, centred on economics. For decades after the Korean War, the North outstripped the South in economic development. The North was rich in natural resources and had always been more industrialised and urbanised than the South. After 1953, thanks to help from the Soviet bloc, North Korea rebuilt the heavy industry factories inherited from the Japanese colonisation and destroyed by the fierce bombing campaign of the United States. According to data collected by the CIA, it was only in 1978 that the per capita gross national product of the South reached the levels of the North. During those years the DPRK grew at a phenomenal rate. It used as much electricity as the South with half the population. From 1965 to 1976 the heavy industry average rate of growth was 14 per cent per annum and even in agriculture productivity was higher in the North than in the South, as was average food intake (3,051 calories per person versus 2,936 calories).[4]

At the beginning of the 1960s, South Korea was a poor country with a per capita income of less than $100 a year. North Korea, with mineral resources and an industrial base, was regarded as the stronger power on the peninsula. Yet the root causes of their different rates of economic development went well beyond the reconstruction after the Korean War or the different stock of natural resources. The South was also suffering from a faulty economic model and the economy had deteriorated in the second half of the 1950s under heavy inflation and high rates of unemployment. From December 1960 to April 1961, the price of rice increased by 60 per cent, while unemployment remained above 23 per cent. At the same time crime rates more than doubled.[5]

While the Marshall Plan was kickstarting the economic miracle of Western Europe, capitalism was failing in the Far East. This was an embarrassment for South Korea, which was clearly losing the race with the North, and a potential danger to the survival of the new regime. It was also an embarrassment for the United States. Suddenly, anti-communist nationalism appeared insufficient to hold the new nation together. It is against this scenario that in 1961 Park Chung Hee launched a military coup in the South, establishing an authoritarian regime. The new dictator fit perfectly in the Cold War dichotomy, opening yet another crevasse between the national identities of the two Koreas. Indeed, Park Chung Hee embodied the antithesis of Kim Il-sung.

In 1942, Park graduated from the Changchun Military Academy of the Manchukuo Imperial Army. He had changed his name to the Japanese Takagi Masao and in 1944 was dispatched as a lieutenant into the Manchukuo Imperial Army. He changed his name again to Okamoto Minoru in order to engage in intelligence activities against Korean guerrillas, most likely led by Kim.

In sharp contrast to Kim Il-sung, Park Chung Hee embraced the notion that Korea was part of the Japanese empire, trading his Korean identity for a Japanese one. The USA welcomed his dictatorship because his life was a testimonial to the false, Cold War interpretation of the Korean conflict: that it had nothing to do with colonisation and decolonisation, but was a battle between good and evil – anti-communism against communism.[6]

The Age of Anti-communist Authoritarianism

Park Chung Hee's military coup was followed by a series of similar military takeovers in Latin America: in Brazil in 1964; in Argentina in 1966 and again in 1976; and in Chile in 1973. All these coups came at the hands of top ranking military officers and all sprang from the politics of the Cold War. These anti-communist, authoritarian, military regimes became close allies of the United States and drew their legitimacy from the struggle to contain the geographical spread of the Soviet model.

These coups were invariably triggered by the poor performance of the national economies due to corruption, mismanagement or socialism, as in Chile under Salvador Allende's rule. Officially, the objective was to bring about economic growth by applying a capitalist system of production, but in reality the coups were instruments to establish the supremacy of the United States. Hence, the economy became priority number one for the South Korean military regime as well as for the Brazilian junta. In both countries, the military leadership appointed well-trained people to manage the transition towards a functioning and successful capitalist economy.

The South Korean model focused on the export market while the Brazilian one followed the classic import substitution formula, the same model that North Korea had embraced.[7] New industries were built in South Korea to target export markets. Incentives for exporters, such as an import licence conditional on export performance, were granted. Tariff exemptions for raw materials and machinery were introduced and more credit to export companies with superior performance was allowed.

As in Brazil, the Park regime used state corporatism to control the unions. As Jorge Dominguez writes,

> It deposed and arrested the union leaders it disliked; it banned some nationwide union federations. It created procedures to interfere regularly with the selection of union leaders and prohibited union political activities. It mandated the creation of joint labour-management committees as the site for collective bargaining.[8]

In this area, however, Park's form of authoritarianism was softer than the one applied in Argentina or Chile.

Overall, the South Korean developmental economic model in the 1960s produced an economic miracle similar to the one that took place in Brazil in the late 1960s and early 1970s. Both countries grew at comparably fast rates during a short time. However, Park's regime was confronted with strong political opposition over controversial foreign policy decisions. In 1964, under the cover of stabilising the economy through a large infusion of capital (about \$800 million in aid), he normalised diplomatic relations with Tokyo, which provoked campus demonstrations in Seoul. In 1965 he took another unpopular decision, sending two Korean divisions to fight alongside US forces in Vietnam, a gesture Washington rewarded by turning South Korea into an important hub for the Vietnam War. Therefore, in the mid-1960s, the largest single source of foreign-exchange earnings for South Korea was its engagement in the Vietnam War. While these funds played a major role in the rapid industrialisation of South Korea, they did not make Park popular.[9] Legislation that allowed labour exploitation and humiliation, including corporal punishment, coupled with Park's pro-Japanese attitude, boosted people's resentment towards him.

At the beginning of the 1970s, losing his grip on the country, Park Chung Hee abandoned the soft style authoritarianism of the previous decade and embraced the harsh model of Argentina and Chile. Not economic growth, but the survival of his regime became his paramount objective. In 1971 he declared a state of emergency and in 1972 suspended the constitution and dissolved the legislature.

Reversal of Fortune

Living with the North Korea of Kim Il-sung as a constant benchmark was not easy for Park. In the 1960s and 1970s, the popularity of the North Korean leader was unquestionable and the South Korean dictator must have observed and studied his rival, seeking strategies to challenge and surpass his political stardom.

In May 1972, Park secretly sent a trusted ally, intelligence chief Lee Hu Rak, to Pyongyang to meet with Kim Il-sung. Lee admiringly voiced his impressions of Kim: 'Quite a guy, very strong, one-man rule!'[10] It was apparent that Kim had achieved what Park was still dreaming of: to indoctrinate society, not just repress it. Park's reshaping of the school curriculum to affect how Korean families related to the nation, a policy he had implemented soon after he took power; his populist messages; the egalitarian ideals he had proposed for universities to seek consensus for his ruling – none of these strategies had produced a national cohesion and identity that could rival Kim Il-sung's North Korea.

Acknowledging such a failure must have enraged and convinced Park that the only way forward for his regime was not more democracy and openness to the world; on the contrary, South Korea should immediately embark on the same path of self-reliance of North Korea, a new vision summarised in the concept of *yushin*. Described as the revitalising reforms system, *yushin* reinforced the authoritarianism of the Park regime. Whoever dissented was arrested, including political leaders, and torture was regularly applied. The atmosphere resembled the violent repression of Latin American military regimes with people being kidnapped and executed. Donald Gregg, the US ambassador in South Korea from 1989 to 1993, describes one episode from that time:

One day in August 1973, Kim Dae Jung, who had loudly and courageously been criticizing the *yushin* system, was kidnapped from a hotel in Tokyo. US Ambassador Philip Habib immediately ordered his aides to find out where the opposition leader was being hidden. Informed the next morning that South Korean agents had seized Kim, Habib rushed to the Blue House, the presidential mansion, to tell Park.

The result was that Kim, on a small boat, tied hand-and-foot and waiting to be thrown into the East Sea, was returned safely to Seoul.[11]

On 26 October 1979, after surviving several previous attempts, Park was assassinated by his close friend Kim Jae-gyu, the director of the Korean Central Intelligence. But the economic miracle he had started carried on, transforming South Korea into a fully industrialised country, naturally with US aid. Park won the economic race against his North Korean enemy, thanks to a little help from his American friend.

As do all developing countries, North and South Korea had got into debt in order to industrialise, importing new technology and even entire factories. The aim went well beyond modernisation: the respective leaderships were engaged in a fierce competition to prove their superiority. The debt piled up and became increasingly difficult to repay. By 1984 South Korea had the third-highest debt of developing countries, while North Korean debt stood at around $2 billion. Unlike South Korea, however, North Korea did not have a guarantor that could act as the lender of last resort.

President Reagan came to the rescue of South Korea with a $4 billion bailout, equivalent to 13 per cent of the total outstanding debt. With this breathing space the South was able to complete the extraordinary effort of modernisation while the North began lagging behind. Well before the fall of the Berlin Wall and the implosion of the Soviet Union, North Korea lost the race to modernise. Yet it maintained a firm grip on its defence north of the thirty-eighth parallel, the Demilitarised Zone.[12]

The DMZ: Korean Surrealism

Nothing more than the Demilitarised Zone (DMZ) illustrates the absurdity of the two Koreas in the twenty-first century. It is a surreal testimonial of the mistakes of the Cold War, proof of the political insanity of the race between the Soviets and the Americans.

For a start, the zone runs near the original demarcation line of 1945, when the Americans cut the Korean peninsula in half. It is worth remembering how it happened. While the Koreans were getting ready to celebrate their liberation after thirty-five years of Japanese colonial rule, inside the US State Department in Washington, DC, two young officers were told to draw a line along the thirty-eighth parallel. They did it on a map taken from *National Geographic*, as if Korea was just a geographical expression. Whatever happened to be south of that line would fall under the jurisdiction of the United States while what was north would be the responsibility of the Soviets.[13] So the lives of millions of people had been sacrificed in a war to contain the new enemy: communism. Families and friends were divided along that imaginary line. The officers acted as Churchill, Stalin and Roosevelt at Yalta, the winning team of World War II, when they split Europe on a map.

The Koreans were never 'liberated'. On the contrary, their punishment for having been a Japanese colony was to be divided, exactly like Germany, which had started the war. Three years later, in 1948, two states emerged almost simultaneously: the Democratic People's Republic of Korea and the Republic of Korea. Because of the geographical position of the Korean peninsula, the thirty-eighth parallel became the de facto frontline of the Cold War.

Today the DMZ is a blast from the past, a place where time froze on 27 July 1953, when the armistice was signed after the devastation of the first conflict of the Cold War, the Korean War. A peace treaty was never signed, perhaps or because the scars of that fratricidal war are still burning on both sides. The symbolism of the DMZ is strong on the southern side. 'From the South you have to go through checkpoints, checkpoints, checkpoints', says Shane Smith, founder of VICE, in his documentary *Inside North Korea*.[14] People also need to sign a document where it is stated that you are entering a 'hostile area' and that you may face the 'possibility of injury or death as a result of enemy action'.[15] The war is a similarly powerful tool of propaganda for the Kim dynasty and the DMZ is its biggest monument. 'People regard it as a warning to how evil the outside world can be', admits a North Korean dissident I interviewed who resides in the United Kingdom. Perhaps because of this role, visiting the DMZ from North Korea is more relaxing. 'Going to the DMZ from the North is a completely different animal than going to the DMZ from the South', explains Smith. Tourists are encouraged to explore the glorious past of North Korea. Panmunjeom, where the armistice was signed in 1953 between the DPRK, China and the

United Nations, represented by the United States, is on the north side. Tourists can visit the Peace Museum, which is more of a war museum of the heroism of the northern troops than a celebration of peace. People are taken around the area by North Korean tour guides, who constantly emphasise the dream of reunification with the South. Do North Koreans really believe this is going to take place?

'The Demilitarised Zone is by far the most densely deployed military zone in the planet', explains Urs Gerber, head of the Swiss delegation of the Neutral Nations Supervisory Commission,[16] which was established in July 1953 to supervise the correct administration of the armistice. The zone is 4 kilometres wide (2 kilometres on each side) and runs from the east to the west coast of the Korean peninsula, very close to the thirty-eighth parallel. Unlike the iron curtain, there is no fence and no barbed wire that runs across the DMZ because it is not necessary. When the armistice was signed about 2,000 mines were placed along the full stretch of the demarcation line by both sides. 'You often hear explosions caused by large animals stepping on a mine', says Gerber.

The DMZ has also become a rare example of un-contaminated fauna and flora in Asia. Mammals such as the rare Amur goral, Asiatic black bear and musk deer inhabit an ecosystem that has thrived without human interference since 1953. There are even reports of tigers, believed to be extinct on the peninsula since before Japanese occupation. It is also a haven for plants, with over 1,600 types of vascular plants and more than 300 species of mushrooms, fungi and lichen believed to be flourishing in the DMZ. The lush vegetation is visible from space. Satellite pictures show on the east side, north of Seoul, a ribbon of bright green, which stands out against the patches of cement of the buildings in the South Korean capital and the deforestation of the North.[17]

This ecological paradise is locked inside a heavily militarised container. The armistice states that only hand guns, no automatic weapons and no artillery are permitted inside the DMZ, yet right outside the 2-kilometre mark on both sides just about any type of weapon is available. 'Since the 1970s there has been a slow re-militarisation of the whole region and the construction of watch towers on both sides', says Gerber. This re-militarisation of the area immediately outside the DMZ has been part of the competition between the two countries. As soon as one side puts up a tower, the other does the same. They have even raced to place the highest pole![18]

The DMZ is where one can truly experience the absurd, childish rivalry between the two nations that should be one. If the South plays Western music in the observation areas for tourists, the North blasts louder its own traditional tunes. Soon the music on both sides becomes so loud that people, disturbed by the cacophony, move away.[19] Due to the proximity of the two visiting sides, the North even built a pristine village to show Koreans and tourists on the other side how well North Koreans live.

As surreal as it can be, the DMZ is a tourist attraction for both sides, a sort of Korean Great Wall, a dystopian Disneyland. At the same time, divided families and friends have visited it as a place of mourning, where they can glance at the land where their loved ones live. Instead of Mickey Mouse and Donald Duck or religious ministers to comfort the sorrow of broken families, there are elite soldiers. They are all tall, handsome and strong, fulfilling the requirement to have mastered martial arts. They stand as statues in pristine uniforms, ready to be photographed or filmed. Tourists love the choreography of the DMZ, they are thrilled to be in what technically still is a war zone, surrounded by all the accessories of war. Meanwhile, Koreans pin on the fences pictures, drawings and letters to their loved ones on the other side, hoping that one day their wishes will be granted.

The cost of the military extravaganza surrounding the two Koreas, of which the DMZ is the jewel in the crown, is phenomenal. For example, South Korea pays for the 28,500 US soldiers stationed in the country, a small contingent in comparison to the 500,000 South Koreans on active duty, plus many more reserves. In 2014 it agreed to pay $866 million to support the US presence, about 5.8 per cent more than in 2013.[20] The American taxpayer also contributes to cover the costs of maintaining the longest armistice in modern times. The US stations troops in Japan to protect the country from North Korea. Approximately 54,000 military personnel, 42,000 dependants, and 800 civil-service employees work at eighty-five facilities in Japan. In addition, the bases employ 25,500 Japanese nationals who work as clerks, fire-fighters, doctors and the like. In 2016, including personnel costs, the US spent roughly $5.5 billion on its Japan presence.[21]

Paradoxically, the heavy militarisation of North and South Korea is not a guarantee that the armistice will hold for ever. In today's tense atmosphere, it represents a serious danger to peace. I interviewed Niklas Swanström, director of the Institute for Security and Development Policy, who believes that a simple incident across the DMZ could easily escalate. In the past, he says, these tense situations were dealt with through hotlines and direct channels, whereas today everything goes through the UN channels. If today there is a confrontation similar to the sinking of the *Cheonan* in 2010, when North Korea sunk the South Korean vessel, Swanström believes it would probably develop into something much worse. The incident happened off an island near the disputed inter-Korean western maritime border.[22] The maritime line of demarcation of the DMZ was never agreed and remains disputed by both sides.

However, what worries experts is the possibility of clashes with Japan, especially in relation to missiles fired over the Japanese territory. Donald Trump has more than once stressed that the United States will protect its ally from North Korea. Ironically, even though Washington has dropped not one, but two atomic bombs on its soil, Japan has developed a special relationship with the United States, being its most important political and economic partner in the Far East, an alliance that has greatly benefited Tokyo. By allowing a platform for American military might, Japan continues to humiliate the leaders of its former colony, North Korea.

Tokyo's Revenge

In the aftermath of World War II, when the Americans occupied Japan, their plan was to build peace and democracy. However, the successes of Mao's long march and the subsequent revolution in China, as well as the Soviet involvement in North Korea, forced them to revise this plan. Washington felt that the overall Cold War political framework had suddenly shifted and new priorities needed to come to the forefront of US foreign policy, that is, anti-communism. Demilitarisation and democratisation, ideals that in 1945 had been welcomed by the defeated and humiliated Japanese population, were put aside. In the process, Americans aligned themselves more and more openly with the conservative and even right-wing elements of Japanese society, including individuals who had been involved in the Japanese war effort.

Charges against prominent figures who had been arrested for war crimes were dropped. The economy was handed back to big capitalists and state bureaucrats. Politicians and other wartime leaders, who had been prevented from holding public office, were gradually reintegrated into politics. While these individuals were 'de-purged', the Americans purged members of the radical left.[23] The consequences of this U-turn soon became apparent. While in 1948, the majority of Japanese people still responded affirmatively when asked if they believed their country was heading in a 'good direction', the next year most of them had changed their minds and showed concern about the future.

In December 1948, however, after the birth of the Democratic People's Republic of Korea, Washington changed its policy and announced that it would modify its economic plan for Japan to focus on the Asian markets. The White House organised a highly publicised mission whose task was to put the country back on its feet. Joseph Dodge, the head of this task force, acted as a dictatorial 'economic czar'. He imposed a conservative plan nicknamed the 'Dodge line', which included a fixed exchange rate of 360 yen to the dollar. Dodge claimed that such a drastic devaluation of the yen was necessary to stabilise the economy. Indeed, the new exchange rate stimulated exports by making Japanese manufactured goods cheaper on the world market. The Dodge line also featured policies to weaken the labour movement through the so-called red purges, watered-down labour laws and 'rationalisations' of enterprises that resulted in the dismissal of thousands and thousands of workers.[24] Overall, these reforms did not produce the expected outcome. They failed to reinvigorate the economy, in part because of the poor conditions of the Asian economy, which limited the surge in exports that the devaluation should have produced. In late April 1950, a US News & World Report described Japan as a country on the 'verge of an economic depression' and labelled the deflation policy 'economic suicide'.[25]

Whether Dodge's policies would eventually have resulted in a true economic depression is a moot point for, in 1950, the outbreak of the Korean War ended the panic in Washington about economic stabilisation. The Korean conflict produced an economic boom in Japan, thanks to the US system of 'special procurements', the US using Japan as its main economic base for the war. The conflict that ravaged Japan's former colony was, as Prime Minister Yoshida and a great many others liked to say, 'a gift of the gods'. At any rate, it was a gift arrived by way of the Americans and reached every corner of Japanese society.[26]

The procurements stimulated most industrial sectors. Starting with metal products and extending to fossil fuels and machinery oils, everything was sourced in Japan, including cloth and finished textile goods, medicines, vehicles, primary metal products, raw materials, non-metallic minerals, electric machines, installation parts, clothing and shoes, building components, lumber and cork products, non-electrical machinery, alcohol and tobacco, paper and paper products, food and rubber products. In addition, the Americans turned to Japan for ammunition, light weapons and napalm bombs. It is somehow ironic that Japan became a big producer of napalm, as the predecessor of this deadly gas was used for the first time in Asakusa, a district of Tokyo, in March 1945, an attack that killed over 100,000 people. Special procurements also extended to services provided for the US forces engaged in the war; repair work on tanks, aircraft and military vehicles was by far the most profitable.[27] Overall, between June 1950 and the end of 1953, special procurements brought an estimated $2.3 billion into Japan, a sum that exceeded the total amount of aid received from the United States between 1945 and 1951. Even after the Korean War ended, military-related US purchases continued under the title 'new special procurements', bringing in an additional $1.75 billion from 1954 to 1956, representing a major portion of the country's 'export' income during these years.[28]

If the development of Japan as an anti-communist ally began in 1948, it was the outbreak of the Korean War on 25 June 1950 that accelerated the urgency in Washington to strengthen Japan and deny both the Soviet Union and the People's Republic of China access to its industrial base and exports. For the Truman and Eisenhower administrations, American foreign economic policy towards Japan became inseparable from the new Cold War political framework. Both presidents worried about the fragility of the US–Japanese alliance, fearing that Japan might have sought an independent course as India had, for example by joining the non-aligned club of nations.

Economic growth and development became the comfort blanket to keep Japan away from other alliances. Both Japan and the United States focused on remedying Japan's ever expanding trade deficit and integrating Japan into the Western trading bloc, the best illustration of which came in 1953, at the end of the Korean War, with the signing of the US–Japan Treaty of Friendship, Commerce, and Navigation, which normalised trade for the first time since 1939. Likewise, the American government did not wish to provoke a Japanese balance-of-payments crisis by forcing Japan to absorb more imports than it could afford to buy. The thinking at the time was that the Japanese economy would ultimately become more like that of the United States, but that it would lag behind for a long time,[29] American post-war planners took for granted that Japan's future markets lay primarily in the less developed countries of Asia, not in the United States or Europe. At a cocktail party in Tokyo, only days before the Korean War began, President Truman's special envoy, John Foster Dulles, blithely but typically told a high-ranking official in the Japanese Finance Ministry that Japan should consider exporting things like, well, cocktail napkins to the United States. Nothing more than this type of product, surely nothing technological and definitely not automobiles. Four years later – with the occupation over and the economy booming thanks to the Korean War – Dulles, then secretary of state in the Eisenhower administration, was still privately and 'frankly' telling Japanese leaders that their country 'should not expect to find a big US market because the Japanese don't make the things we want. Japan must find markets elsewhere for the goods they export'.[30] John Foster Dulles would soon be proven wrong.

From 1955 onwards, there was a huge surge in Japanese exports to the United States, growing at a rate of 10 per cent per annum through the 1970s. Of course, this was due to the key role that Japan played in supplying the US Army in Korea and then in Vietnam.

In the second half of the 1950s, while North Korea was licking its war wounds and the South Korean economy was struggling to grow, the Japanese economy began taking off, thanks to the extraordinary benefits of the Korean War. Japan's alliance with the United States and economic supremacy over its former colony did not go unnoticed in Pyongyang; it cemented the belief that self-reliance was the only way forward and that Japan and the United States would continue to be a constant threat to the new nation. As we shall see, this belief facilitated the notion among North Koreans that they needed to achieve nuclear capability.

Chapter 3

Survival Economy

North Korea perfectly fits the Cold War stereotype of the brainwashed nation, victim of a ruthless and demented leader in cahoots with an equally paranoid ruling elite. Unlike Cuba, where the music and sandy beaches clash with the dehumanising images of totalitarianism, North Korea, with its gigantic military parades, is a country that people have no problem thinking of as a place that belongs in one of Ian Fleming's Bond novels: the stronghold of an evil and crazed power whose aim is to annihilate the free world. Naturally, this is not the case. The scenarios of the 007 series never existed; nonetheless, this image strikes a chord with many.

The stereotype of the irrational, evil nature of the North Korean regime reinforces the post-Cold War narrative that, at both economic and political levels, Western capitalism is so superior to any other system that only evil and crazy forces would oppose it. And because communism is capitalism's natural enemy, North Korea must be a communist country, with an economy built on the blueprint of the old Soviet model.

The simplistic nature of such analysis is apparent: if the Soviet system was faulty, as indeed it was, how is it possible that almost thirty years after its collapse, North Korea, a mere replica, still stands? The politics of repression cannot explain the survival of the North Korean regime, nor the fact that communist Cuba still exists. Nor is the religious fervour that the *juche* ideology produces sufficient to justify the endurance of the North Korean system. Both Cuba and North Korea must have done something to build a resilience that the Soviet Union and the Eastern European bloc lacked. To understand the uniqueness of North Korea, we have to go back to the aftermaths of World War II and the Korean War, when the nation and its regime took shape.

The Juche Economy

Splitting up the Korean peninsula created a massive economic shock. While as a single country Korea had enough resources to become a wealthy nation, divided it struggled to make ends meet. For a start, two-thirds of the population lived in the South (15.6 million of the 23.5 million) and one-third in the North (7.9 million), so the division produced a demographic imbalance. All the natural resources, including the coal deposits, were located in the North, while the South has always been agricultural. The heavy industry and the bulk of the energy sector was in the North, which produced about

92 per cent of electricity for the entire peninsula. The bulk of the light industry, including the textile sector, was in the South. Cutting the country in half produced serious economic imbalances that crippled growth in both Koreas; the South had food but no energy while the North had energy but no food.

In the South, industrialisation took place under the banner of capitalism and amid the exploitation, often inhuman, of the labour force, which included corporal punishment under Park.[1] A glimpse of the barbaric practices inside their factories could be seen in the Chinese Economic Zones, where many industrialists moved to in the 1980s when legislation at home put an end to excessive labour exploitation.[2] South Korea belonged to the Asian Tigers, alongside Singapore, Hong Kong and Taiwan. From the 1950s to the 1980s, these were authoritarian countries that created a new type of government, the 'development state'.[3] Legitimacy was not necessarily connected to democratic elections but to the ability of the leaders to sustain uninterrupted economic growth.[4] Indeed, this is the model that, after 1989, Deng Xiao Pin applied to the modernisation of China.

In 1948 North Korea emerged as a totalitarian state, but took a different economic route from South Korea; it embarked on the creation of a centrally planned economy. Kim Il-sung sought the help and support of Moscow and Beijing, North Korea's communist neighbours, to rebuild the North. The full involvement of these two countries lasted until the mid-1950s, when North Korea began distancing itself from both of them.

Interestingly, the *juche* economy, a ramification of the *juche* doctrine, was never properly formulated or spelled out, possibly because it is impossible to reconcile economics with an act of faith. In the absence of a proper socio-economic doctrine, the *juche* economy was often improvised and formulated as a reaction to unexpected events. Its primary task was not to bring about economic development or to prove the superiority of the communist model over the capitalist one, but to guarantee the survival, at any cost and at any price, of the North Korean state. And because such a state was intimately intertwined with the Kim dynasty, the *juche* economy became an instrument to protect the political status quo.

Nothing can be further from the rigid Soviet economic planning than the *juche* economy. As Byung-Yeon Kim pointed out in his brilliant book *Unveiling the North Korean Economy*, even if North Korea wanted to, it could not have planned ahead because 'it was incapable of creating, collecting and processing data', lacking properly trained technocrats.[5] Unlike the Bolsheviks and the Chinese revolutionary elite, the North Korean leadership – those who had fought and won a war of independence against Japan – were uneducated people, often of peasant origin, and orphans raised to protect the family-nation. They were great warriors but knew very little about the infrastructure required to build a solid economy.

The *juche* ideology was never a viable alternative system to capitalism but more akin to the religion of a new sect. The legitimacy of reforms came from an act of faith of the people, not from an ideological choice. This explains why the leadership promoted and used mass mobilisation to justify major economic changes. Unlike in China, a country with a strong tradition of mass mobilisation, in North Korea manifestations of popular support were staged and expressed as a religious faith in the leadership, instead of a real involvement in the shaping of the future of the masses.

Against this background, the failure of North Korea to maximise the use of its own resources and to promote economic development cannot be attributed to the inefficiency of the Soviet model. Paradoxically, the absence of proper planning, of a 'communist' vision of the future, coupled with the religious nature of the leadership's popular support, gave the North Korean economy a flexibility and adaptability, a resilience to major shocks, that saved the country from total collapse on more than one occasion, including the implosion of the Soviet Union.

The Perfect Famine Storm

When the Berlin Wall came down, the world rejoiced at the victory of the West over an evil empire, as Ronald Reagan had described the Soviet bloc.[6] In the midst of such euphoria, nobody paid attention to the impact of the USSR's sudden decline on the geopolitical equilibrium of the Cold War. Politicians ignored the fact that entire nations, which had been instrumental to the balancing games of the two superpowers, woke up to a new reality wherein their superpatron either had vanished or was no longer interested in them. Countries like Somalia imploded for exactly these reasons. Today, we still live with the consequences of this indifference, which was a very serious mistake. If we do accept this criticism, the North Korean famine of the second half of the 1990s cannot exclusively be attributed to the regime's absurd totalitarianism. Other factors, such as the mismanagement of the post-Cold War years as well as the climatic changes triggered by global warming, also contributed to this catastrophe.

Like Cuba, North Korea benefited from Soviet imports of cheap energy. When almost overnight they disappeared, the country had to shut down several factories. Because the national economy greatly relied on heavy industry, higher oil prices immediately caused a contraction in GDP. A similar phenomenon took place in Cuba. In addition, with the Soviet Union being a significant importer of North Korean and Cuban products, its disintegration further contracted the economy of both countries. While in due course Fidel Castro was able to rely on cheap Venezuelan oil, North Korea could not. Yet it was not because of access to cheap oil that one economy survived while the other collapsed: the differentiating factor was the weather.

Unlike Cuba, North Korea is a country with long, freezing winters and vast forests. Without fuel, people began cutting trees to burn for heat. This practice was allowed and even encouraged. Indeed, as early as the 1980s, to increase food production, the *juche* agricultural edicts prompted peasants to clear and plant along steep slopes, without the environmental consideration that proper planning would have produced. Between 1980 and 2000, forest cover in North Korea declined from 74 per cent to 58 per cent, while agricultural land increased from 17 per cent to 23 per cent.[7] Intensified clearing of forests and of marginal land for agriculture produced vast land degradation. In the mid-1990s, when North Korea was hit for several years in a row by extreme weather conditions – including massive floods, tidal waves and droughts – this land degradation amplified their impact and eventually led to a catastrophic reduction in food output.

The collapse of the agricultural sector was, therefore, a human-made disaster, as was Mao's Great Leap Forward. Though it is difficult to know how many people died in the famine, reasonable estimates put the number of victims of starvation at around 600,000, about 2–2.5 per cent of the population of the DPRK. After the collapse of the Soviet Union, while China was opening up to Western capitalism and amid a famine of biblical proportion, the totalitarian North Korean regime did not implode. How did the leadership survive?

Informal Economy

When the DPRK was founded, Kim Il-sung introduced the classic communist model of state control of natural resources.[8] In agriculture, the production system relied on collective farms and cooperatives, while the distribution took place via a ration system known as the Public

Distribution System.[9] When the central government lost its ability to supply food through this system,[10] it made a decision that its Chinese and Soviet counterparts probably would not have taken: it let people trade food.

The *juche* economy was sufficiently vague to allow the sudden marketisation of the economy, and the *juche* ideology was such a strong religion that people simply accepted the fact that, from now on, the burden of survival was on their shoulders. It is important to stress that the collapse of the Public Distribution System was directly linked to the starvation of hundreds of thousands of people who could not feed themselves otherwise. Even though the state had let them down, the North Korean population continued to have a religious faith in the regime and used their ingenuity to survive.

At the ground level, the transition towards a semi-private agriculture was made easy by the faulty nationalisation of resources, which had not been conducted properly from the outset. In the absence of proper planning, the agricultural sector lacked a strong built-in rigidity, which turned out to be a great advantage for its survival and for the maintenance of the political system. People could work small plots of land near their homes and trade the produce without running into red tape or bureaucratic roadblocks.

The marketisation of the economy was accompanied by other measures. In addition to foreign aid, which poured into the country due to the seriousness of the humanitarian crisis, the leadership decided to attract foreign capital, following the example of China. In the late 1990s it established North Korea's Special Economic Zones. The first one was near the Chinese border, in the Rajin-Seonbong region and the second was near the Demilitarised Zone, on the Kumgang Mountain. As part of an agreement with the government of South Korea, Korean companies were granted a special licence to manufacture for the export market in these areas using the North Korean labour force.[11] North Korean workers with specialised skills were also dispatched abroad to earn hard currencies.

In an effort to cope with the collapse of the Public Distribution System and to offset the drastic fall in fiscal revenues, the leadership decentralised the already poor planning system. With the marketisation of the economy, planning was turned upside down, implemented from the bottom up instead of from the top down as in the Soviet Union.

The emergency measures did not go as far as Deng's reform in China – once the economy was normalised no further steps were taken, so, for example, decollectivisation never took place. Why? Because every economic measure was put in place to maintain the status quo, not to open up the economy. The informal economy remained and began contaminating the rest of the economy, building a further resilience inside the system that enabled it to weather the sanctions of the second decade of the twenty-first century. But before we analyse this aspect of the North Korean economy, let's look at the other strategy used by the North Korean leadership to survive the tragic 1990s: the gift economy.

The Gift Economy

Fervour for the *juche* doctrine and for the Kim dynasty may have fooled the general population, but it was never going to work with the ruling elite. Luckily, in the 1970s, when Kim Jong-il emerged as the future leader, he established a system of loyalty based on the gift policy. He simply showered those who supported him with expensive luxury presents and purged those who opposed him. It was the tried and tested carrot and stick approach. The objective of the gift policy was 'to win the hearts of senior officials. The recipients believe that the supreme leader thinks highly of them. [...] people develop a strong sense of belonging and feel they would die for their leader', explains Kang Myung Do, a defector who, as a former North Korean official, was involved in the distribution of gifts.[12]

The intensification of the gift policy in the 1990s allowed Kim Jong-il to retain sufficient loyalty to weather the traumatic years of the famine and the following decade of economic stagnation. The creation of the gift policy was totally independent from the economy of the DPRK and it was controlled by the leader, in a fashion that resembled the mythical chairman's fund of Arafat, a personal treasury that the leader of the Palestinian Liberation Army accumulated and used to maintain power.

Under Kim Jong-il, North Korea developed two economies, explains Kim Kwang Jin, a defector who was an official of North Korea and has an extensive knowledge of how these economies worked. One was the general public economy and the other was the royal court economy, a de facto secret fund. Established by Kim Jong-il, the latter became the financial foundation of the Kim dynasty. Kim Jong-il diverted public funds towards the royal court economy, money he could use without the party's approval for gift politics, to garner substantial support personally and for military projects, including the nuclear program. Under Kim Jong-il the royal court economy grew bigger than the people's economy, about 60 per cent of the entire economy of North Korea.[13]

According to a former official interviewed for the documentary *Money & Power in North Korea*, the engine that siphoned funds towards the royal court economy was an ad hoc organisation called Room 39. It controlled all kinds of businesses: trading firms, mines, factories, foreign currencies, restaurants, farms, livestock producers and more. The foreign currency collected by Room 39 was kept separate from the state budget and went directly to the supreme leader, who used it as he pleased. The cash, mostly yen, US dollars and euros, was stored in the party headquarters, near where Room 39 was located, in central Pyongyang.[14]

The distribution of gifts took place at various times during the year, but always for the new year and for the leader's birthday. The procurement was left to buyers who travelled everywhere to shop: the most common destinations were Germany, Austria, Guangdong province in China and Macau. Kim Jong Ryul, a defector who was a gift buyer for twenty years, specialising in luxury cars for North Korean senior officials, says he was always given specific instructions as the gifts were chosen according to the rank of the recipients and to what had been given before. Gift politics became so engraved into the loyalty system that receiving a less precious gift could have been interpreted as a sign that the recipient had lost favour. 'You needed to give something better than before, otherwise a present could have had a negative effect', concluded Kang Myung Do.[15]

A major source of foreign currency for the royal court economy was the sale of weapons abroad, which was estimated to have netted around $1 billion.[16] Buyers would visit North Korean factories, but the sales and transactions took place in Macau where the foreign exchange originated. Room 39 had an office in Macau for this specific task. The buyers came from Southeast Asia, the Middle East and Africa.

If the shambolic management of the North Korean economy was a key factor in the economy's adaptability to changing circumstances, eventually the lack of a proper economic vision became a burden. At the turn of the millennium, the reactive nature of economic reforms became conducive to corruption. It is within this context that we have to place the widely publicised execution of Kim Jong-un's uncle Jang Sung-taek.

The Purge

Most consumer goods in North Korea are imported or smuggled from China and, indeed, this represents the largest source of revenue for North Koreans. Facing the collapse of the economy in the 1990s, Kim Jong-il introduced a system of licences for import-export. Companies began competing with each other to get the *waku*, the trade licence. The *waku* was used as an essential instrument to gain and cement loyalties among the elite, to maintain the balance of power among the powerful institutions – the army, the party and the cabinet – and to divert funds away from the people's economy towards the elite.[17]

Mimicking the model of the royal court economy, institutions and officials used the *waku* to establish their own private treasury. The concession of the licence, in fact, commanded a 'donation' or 'commission' to the institution or the official who had been instrumental in getting it. In this way, the link between the state apparatus and the companies formed a relationship of interdependency and mutual support.

North Korean import-export companies used mispricing of invoices to raise the money to pay the *waku*'s commission. This is how a North Korean dissident journalist describes import mispricing:

There is a wide range of irregularities in imports. For example, if you are importing 100,000 dollars worth of equipment, the book will have an import price of 200,000 dollars and the difference will be divided among those involved in the business, i.e. the person in charge of the institution which granted the *Waku*, the person in charge of the import and the person in charge of finance.[18]

Mispricing of imports is a technique widely used in the free market to evade taxation. While it is difficult to manipulate general sales items, such as groceries and commodities, whose prices are well known, it is easy to inflate the import prices of inexpensive items. In the case of North Korea, mispricing is even easier because most consumer products sold inside the country are made in China and the number of importers is very limited, so the risk of being exposed is small.

Mispricing of export products happens in a similar fashion. In North Korea goods are officially sold at a lower price than the world market, but the buyer pays the right price. The difference can even be collected in cash and used to pay the commission. 'Export rights to underground resources such as gold, anthracite, and iron ore in the DPRK are exclusively owned by the 38th Office of the Workers' Party, the military, and special agencies', the same journalist writes. 'When they export national resources, they declare how much they sold per tonne in the invoice, but they take more and pocket the difference.'[19]

Jang Sung-taek was involved in this corruption ring.[20] A North Korean dissident blogger writes:

he said that he sold anthracite coal to China at a low price. At the time, the international price was around 130 dollars per tonne and was sold for 75 dollars per tonne. Did the North Korean trade workers sell foolishly and cheaply? Not at all. The 75 dollars is just an accounting price. In fact, it was common knowledge that Jang Sung-taek and his entourage had personally received from the sale more than 25 dollars per tonne. Last year, North Korea's anthracite coal exports amounted to nearly 1.4 billion dollars, so a minister who monopolized exports of anthracite coal would have collected hundreds of millions of dollars.[21]

The corruption ring built around the *waku* is a corollary of the royal court economy; it drains money and resources away from the people's economy to feed an increasingly greedy elite.

North Korea is one of the poorest countries on the planet...Actually, billions of dollars evaporated due to the difference between the import/export price and the real price, and it turns into luxury apartments, luxury goods and luxury services in Pyongyang. Inside offices in charge of trade in various leadership and government institutions there is an abundant number of children and relatives of the senior elite that make sure that this system runs smoothly.[22]

Not any longer. The arrival of the new leader, Kim Jong-un, was followed by a series of purges and swift executions at top levels aimed at crippling the corruption system and freeing foreign exchange to soften the blow of economic sanctions on the economy. Many believe that Jang Sung-taek was at the centre of this corruption web. In 2015, 'North Korea's largest export item was anthracite coal at 1,373.71 million dollars. The largest import item was oil, 591.31 million dollars. Jang Sung-taek and his entourage controlled these products, accounting for more than 30% of total trade', concluded the dissident blogger.[23] The purge hit at the heart of this vast network. According to North Korean sources, 4,000 people have been executed or exiled since the execution of Jang Sung-taek.[24]

Crime and Punishment in the DPRK

Deep down, North Korea maintains totalitarian and feudal elements that make the regime repulsive to Westerners. Indeed, the DPRK is not governed by the rule of law. Crime and punishment follows a set of rules that are very different from those applied in Western democracies, as is well illustrated by the swift execution of Jang Sung-taek and army chief Ri Ying Ho, two powerful men who had been very close to Kim Jong-il. As with economics, the justice system is constructed to keep the regime in power, not to provide justice to everybody. While institutions are instruments to preserve the status quo, people are all expendable, even those very close to the leader. Nobody is safe, not even the elite. This is particularly true today under the rule of Kim Jong-un. According to Evan Medeiros, President Obama's chief Asia adviser,

> [Kim Jong-il's] approach to managing élites appeared to be more incentive-based than coercion-based, making sure that they all got goodies and spoils. [...] The son's approach appears to be 'If you screw with me, I'm just going to kill you – and I'm going to kill you in a really nasty way'.[25]

Everybody concurs that executing Jang Sung-taek was an extraordinary act of boldness. The purge was aimed at protecting the leadership in a very difficult transition. The killing of Kim Jong-nam, Kim Jong-un's older brother, had similar motivations. Though he lived in exile and had no desire or status to challenge his brother – Kim Jong-il had judged him unfit to rule the country because he was too Westernised and lacked the qualities of a good leader – Kim Jong-nam had expressed criticisms vis-à-vis his brother's rule, describing him as just a figurehead. In February 2017, Kim Jong-nam was killed at Kuala Lumpur International Airport, in Malaysia, with the nerve agent VX, a tasteless, odourless chemical weapon. According to media reports, he may have been killed because he was ready to defect or to cooperate with foreign intelligence services. However, such news was never made public inside the DPRK; state media mentioned only that a diplomat had died of heart failure in Malaysia.

As a general rule, however, the North Korean regime purposely publicises and stages executions and assassinations to scare people, to intimidate those who may be thinking of challenging the ruler. The punishment must fit the crime and any crime against the leadership is treason and blasphemy. The divinity that the *juche* creed constructed around the Kim dynasty explains people's acceptance that their lives can and will be sacrificed for the good of the leader. This is a crucial point of divergence between the DPRK and the democratic system.

Further, because justice is not equal for everybody, it will be more or less lenient according to certain factors, the most important of which is the *songbun,* the caste system.

There are two types of crimes in North Korea – ordinary crimes and crimes of a political nature – and they are clearly distinguished in the North Korean criminal justice system. Within this context, *songbun* classification plays an important role in North Korea's laws and legal system, leading to judgments and sentences that are discriminatory. Those of higher *songbun* typically get lighter sentences than those who commit similar crimes but are from the lower *songbun* classes. Indeed, the North Korean penal code recognizes political and class distinctions.[26]

The 2017 Human Rights Watch report on North Korea stated the following:

North Korea discriminates against individuals and their families on political grounds in key areas such as employment, residence, and schooling through *songbun,* the country's socio-political classification system that from its creation grouped people into [five classes] such as 'loyal,' 'wavering,' or 'hostile' classes. This classification has been restructured several times, but continues to enable the government to privilege or disadvantage people based largely on family background, personal performance, and perceived political loyalty.

However, pervasive corruption enables some room to manoeuvre around the strictures of the *songbun* system, even while it burdens people as government officials regularly demand and receive bribes from those seeking permissions, pursuing market activities, or wishing to travel inside or outside the country.[27]

Paradoxically, bribes have reduced the rigidity and inequality of the caste system. This relaxation began during the famine, in the mid-1990s. As informal markets have penetrated the economy, bribes have softened the *juche* crime and punishment system. Particularly for minor types of crime and in the countryside, people can easily bribe the police and get away without being arrested, as proven by the investigation conducted by the *Washington Post* among North Korean dissidents. Here is the testimony of a former North Korean drug dealer who escaped in 2014:

> My main business was selling ice (methamphetamine). I think that 70 or 80 percent of the adults in Hoeryong city were using ice. My customers were just ordinary people. Police officers, security agents, party members, teachers, doctors. Ice made a really good gift for birthday parties or for high school graduation presents. It makes you feel good and helps you release stress, and it really helps relations between men and women. My 76-year-old mother was using it because she had low blood pressure, and it worked well. Lots of police officers and security agents would come to my house to smoke, and of course I didn't charge them – they were my protection. They would come by during their

lunch break, stop by my house. The head of the secret police in my area was almost living at my house.[28]

According to the crime committed, if found guilty, people are assigned to different prison systems. Those who have committed small crimes, petty thieves for example, end up in labour training centres, *rodong danryondae*. According to Human Rights Watch, inmates may also be people suspected of involvement in unauthorised trading schemes or shirking work at state-owned enterprises for more than six months. The *rodong danryeondae* are de facto forced labour detention facilities. Inmates spend half a day working and the remaining time being rewired to the system – listening to propaganda. Though discipline is strict and violence is common, security is light, and inmates have escaped from these labour camps.[29] More serious criminals end up in tougher labour camps: *gyohwaso,* correctional re-education centres. Those convicted of smuggling or of minor political infractions, such as watching or selling South Korean films, will find themselves here. Generally, food is scarce and the inmates endure forced labour wherever it is needed, from the copper mines to the rice fields.[30]

But the most brutal treatment is reserved for the dissidents. UN officials estimate that between 80,000 and 120,000 people are imprisoned in political prison camps known as *kwanliso,* all operated by North Korea's National Security Agency.[31] According to Human Rights Watch:

these camps are characterized by systematic abuses, including meagre rations that imperil health and can lead to starvation, virtually no medical care, lack of proper housing and clothes, regular mistreatment including sexual assault and torture by guards, and public executions. Political prisoners face backbreaking forced labour, including in logging, mining, and agricultural.[32]

Political prisoners are sent to detention centres with their families. Three generations are considered guilty by association, known in Korean as *yeonjwaje*, so people end up in prison camps with their parents, children and siblings' families. As in the ancient Korean feudal system, the state discriminates against sons and grandsons of criminals and political opponents. 'If you make problems, then your whole family gets punished. That's why people don't want to make any trouble. If I get punished for my wrongdoing, that's one thing. But it's my whole family that would be put at risk if I did something', says the drug dealer interviewed by the *Washington Post*.[33] Perhaps the guilty-by-association principle is one of the major deterrents to political dissent as people do not want to harm their family, especially their parents. Both North and South Koreans are extremely conformist and opposing your parents is unthinkable.

As in every country, foreigners visiting North Korea must accept the country's justice system, no matter how brutal it is. In the summer of 2017, Otto Warmbier, a University of Virginia student who had been arrested in January 2016 and found guilty of 'a hostile act against the state' for trying to remove a propaganda poster from the wall of a hotel in Pyongyang, was brought home. He was in a coma and died less than a week later. A Western diplomat who at the time resided in Pyongyang said that he had heard rumours Otto Warmbier may have also been involved in some kind of religious activity. The death of the young student prompted the US State Department to ban Americans from travelling to North Korea.

Warmbier was not the first American to be arrested in the DPRK. In the past ten years, sixteen Americans have been detained and released, yet none suffered the same treatment. The North Koreans claimed Warmbier had contracted botulism while in captivity, but doctors in Cincinnati who treated him did not find traces of botulism. The family claimed he had been beaten and tortured, but again doctors could not find evidence of this brutality. Foreign detainees represent a value for North Korea because they can be important bargaining chips, so they are generally not beaten. Because the family refused to let the doctors perform an autopsy, we will never know the true cause of the coma and the death of Otto Warmbier. We can only speculate. Several experts on North Korea suspect that he got sick in prison and was given a massive and fatal dose of medication that led to the coma. As for the failure to release him through informal diplomatic channels, Evan Osnos reports in *The New Yorker* of a conversation he had in Pyongyang with a Pak Song-il, a North Korean diplomat, about Warmbier's case.

Negotiators for the Warmbier family, such as Bill Richardson, the former governor of New Mexico, had been frustrated in their efforts, and I asked Pak why the government had stonewalled them. Pak blamed an Obama Administration decision, in July, 2016, to impose personal sanctions on Kim Jong un and other top officials. 'Obama blacklisted our leaders, and smeared them by name,' Pak said. 'At that point, we could not accept it. We cut off the New York channel [the only direct line between the two nations] and we adopted wartime measures. From then on, we said, the situation will stay as is.'[34]

The Obama administration made a terrible mistake due to the lack of knowledge and understanding of the DPRK. The United States does not have any formal representation or channel of communication in North Korea as it does not recognise the regime. Normally, in these situations Sweden handles US affairs, but there is no evidence that the Swedish government was involved in the release of Otto Warmbier. Without diplomatic channels, the young American was left alone to deal with a feudal justice system that eventually led to his death. His life was lost due to incompetence, but hundreds of thousands more lives could be lost in the future because the channels of communication between the DPRK and the USA have been cut.

Chapter 4

Status Quo: The Korean Model of Development

The endurance of North Korea springs from several characteristics that set this country apart from the rest of the world, from the religious ideology of *juche* to the strong collective identity of North Koreans, to the perception of the state as a family and of the leader as a father. These traits appear to the globalised and sophisticated Westerner as signs of political repression, harking back to the darkest period of Stalin's rule. To support this comparison, the media has produced endless proof of the barriers the regime has erected around its own citizens, existential walls to prevent them from interacting with foreigners. This isolation fuels the belief that people are prisoners in their own country. This is not true.[1] Perhaps the failure of the international media to present a comprehensive picture of this nation rests in the fact that they operate outside the domain of religion and faith. International journalists cannot conceive North Korea as a sect, similar to Scientology, and prefer to invoke the comparison with a totalitarian regime, such as the Soviet Union.

In recent years, the Cold War dynamic and propaganda has been dusted off and adapted to globalisation in order to present the DPRK as a brutal regime. However, North Korea is very different from Stalin's Soviet Union or Maoist China. But, like any other country and regime, it cannot remain static; it needs to grow and adapt to changes taking place outside its borders. This is the biggest challenge the leadership and the nation faces today. History tells us that the Soviet system was too rigid to survive while the Chinese system was sufficiently flexible to reform. Everybody would agree that present-day China is very different from the China of the 1990s. The key question is: will North Korea follow in the footsteps of Beijing and become something else or fail miserably as Moscow did?

Maintaining the status quo, the survival of the regime, is paramount today as it was in the 1950s. Nobody will dispute this statement. But one could say the same of the US and European democracies: no political system will accept out of hand being replaced by a new one! At least in this respect, North Korea is no different from any other country. But, unlike Western democracies, it is the leadership that brings about changes, not the ballot. Kim Il-sung and Kim Jong-il managed to weather major crises, including the collapse of the agricultural system in the second half of the 1990s. Kim Jong-un does not have an easier task and, while battling with sanctions, he is attempting to improve the economy.

Why Sanctions Have Not Worked

Most of what we hear or read about North Korea sounds surreal or paradoxical, so we should not be surprised to learn that during the first years of his rule, Kim Jong-un's best ally was the system of economic sanctions aimed at stopping the nuclear program and potentially toppling the regime. To a population that regards self-reliance as an integral part of life – like the air they breathe – the UN sanctions are just a challenge that must be overcome, not a reason to abandon a nuclear program that is considered the jewel in the crown of the Kim dynasty and a source of immense pride for the entire nation. Vladimir Putin seems to understand North Koreans better than Donald Trump. At a September 2017 meeting with President Xi in Xiamen, China, Putin stressed that sanctions of any kind are useless and ineffective and that the North Koreans would eat grass, but they would not abandon their nuclear program.[2]

Because the sanctions have not worked, people have attributed this to Kim Jong-un's ability to offset their impact. Indeed, recently the North Korean economy has been performing quite well. According to the Central Bank of South Korea, in 2016 it grew 3.9 per cent, driven primarily by the mining and energy sectors.[3] This is the highest rate of growth in seventeen years. Living conditions have also improved due to the limited market reforms that Kim Jong-un has introduced. As discussed in the next section, these reforms have allowed the informal economy to grow and wages to rise. 'Over the last four years there have been many improvements in living standards', explains the European diplomat I interviewed who left Pyongyang at the end of October 2017.

> For example, the supply of electricity in the capital has become more steady, in 2017 we hardly had any power cuts. Despite the sanctions, people have more disposable income and feel that they are getting wealthier. Four years ago, who could have thought that North Koreans would buy ebikes? Today you see them commonly in the streets of Pyongyang.

Recently the number of ebikes has increased to multiple thousands in Pyongyang. The bikes cost between $300 and $500 and the batteries are usually taken to people's homes to be recharged. A 2017 Unicef report on the living conditions of women and children in the DPRK confirms that several improvements have been achieved:

> DPR Korea has a well-articulated network of social services reaching down to the village level, and has made significant progress in increasing enrolment in both primary and secondary education, as well as decreasing mortality due to preventable causes. [...] Overall infant, child, and maternal mortality have decreased significantly.[4]

In an interview with al Jazeera, Professor Byung-Yeon Kim concurs that the North Korean economy is healthier than in the past and adds that since Kim Jong-un took power four years ago, the biggest engine of economic growth has been foreign trade and the proliferation of domestic consumer markets, also known as informal markets.[5] In 2016, North Korea's biggest trade partner by far was China, which accounted for 92.5 per cent of total trade, followed by Russia with just 1.2 per cent and other countries with a total of 6.3 per cent. To get an idea of the importance of China for the DPRK economy, in 2016, trade with China amounted to $6.5 billion, with exports and imports of $2.92 billion and $3.6 billion respectively.[6]

Trade has primarily boosted the construction industry and the energy industry. In recent years, North Korea has built additional power plants and renewed the power transmission lines, no doubt explaining why there are fewer power cuts. The economy and the sanctions hinge on the energy sector. In 2017, under pressure from the United States, China agreed to ban all imports of coal and to expel North Korean companies operating in China. It is unclear if these measures will have the desired impact, however. It is also unclear if China will ever agree to hit North Korea with a proper oil embargo.

North Korea does not produce any oil and imports about 1 billion tonnes per year, more than half of this from China. The other major oil exporter is Russia. Chinese oil is imported through a pipeline. If China agrees to shut the pipeline, it would cut between 40 and 50 per cent of North Korean oil consumption. The negative impact on the economy would be felt immediately, explains Professor Byung-Yeon Kim.[7] So

Donald Trump is right when he claims that China has the power to hit the North Korean economy hard. Yet an oil embargo would mean that China has abandoned its ally in Pyongyang, an ally that provides a buffer against the presence of US troops on its border. Those who know China and North Korea concur it is highly unlikely this will happen. Let's also not forget that China is the USA's largest trade partner, so it has strong bargaining power.

Not everybody agrees that an oil embargo would cripple the North Korean economy. The US–Korea Institute at Johns Hopkins University published an article explaining why an oil price hike would be more effective than a full embargo.

[The] import value of mineral oil and oil products from China in 2016 was only less than half of such imports in 2012, when they stood at 773 million USD. Measured in tons, the amount in 2016 was 799,000 while it was 705,000 in 2012. The imported amount of oil from China has remained more or less stable, but it now costs only half as much as it did a few years ago. An increase in world market prices for oil would have a much more serious effect on North Korean oil imports than most sanctions. We also find that at current prices, with cash reserves of, for example, 2 billion USD, the North Korean government could easily cover their oil imports for the next five years without exporting a single item.[8]

So far the North Korean leadership has been able to shield the population from the impact of energy sanctions, as the European diplomat explains.

In April 2016 the price of fuel went up 80 per cent overnight, then a few months later again another 20 per cent increase. From March to September the price of petrol doubled and yet the impact on the economy has been nil. Taxis cost the same, everything costs the same. Why? The only explanation is that taxis must get subsidised fuel, perhaps the government gives taxi drivers fuel coupons. They can do that because there are virtually no private cars in North Korea, all transportation belongs to the government. But what is remarkable is that the doubling of prices at the pump has not triggered inflation. So far, the regime has succeeded in sheltering the economy from the impact of the sanctions on energy. It is a smart move because as long as people are satisfied and as long as they feel that their lives are getting better, they remain 100 per cent behind the leadership.

As in the rest of the world, the survival of the regime is intertwined with the economic health of the nation, a fact that the Kims have long known. Kim Jong-un has even changed the old motto 'the army first' to 'the economy and the army first'. This is another major difference with the Soviet system. By the time Moscow came under serious economic pressure, the Nomenclatura had severed all ties with the population and thought only of its own survival.

A dissident who escaped in 2014 confirms the spreading of an informal market economy:

> I had an aunt in Pyongyang who sold beans in the market there. I would buy what she needed from various farmers and get it to her. I'd pay people to pack up the beans into sacks, pay porters to take them to the station, get them onto the train. You have to smooth the way with money. My uncle is in the military, so his position provided protection for my aunt's business. Of course, my aunt was the main earner in the house. It's the women who can really make money in North Korea.[9]

Indeed, women are heavily involved in the informal market economy.

Offsetting the sanctions is expensive. 'To maintain people's perception that the sanctions are not biting, it is costing the state a lot of money', says the European diplomat. Where does the leadership get the funds to subsidise fuel?

> What the government is doing is cutting expenditure in infrastructure investments or their renewal, that is the easiest and quickest way to save money in the short term. So in the long run the sanctions will produce a deterioration in infrastructure, but that is all. The country is self-sufficient in food, the majority of the people live on subsistence, so people will not starve again.

As Ann Fifield notes in her *Washington Post* article, 'North Korea technically has a centrally planned economy, but now people's lives revolve around the market. No one expects the government to provide things anymore. Everyone has to find their own way to survive.'[10]

One sector where the sanctions are hurting the regime is banking. 'It has become increasingly difficult for the state to hold an efficient banking system. I can see that this is the sector where the sanctions are indeed giving the leadership a hard time', reveals a Chinese trader I interviewed in October 2017. The European diplomat adds, 'So far, the leadership is using strategies to overcome these problems, even if it means dealing in cash'.

In the second half of 2017, the United States began exploring the possibility of imposing secondary sanctions on countries, companies and individuals that continue to do business with the DPRK, including China. However, analysts concur that the impact of secondary sanctions would be less than a straightforward oil embargo from China, while the cost of implementing them would be much higher. Secondary sanctions will also require daily monitoring, which takes time and resources.

Historically, economic sanctions have rarely achieved any change. In the case of North Korea they may simply convince the leadership to strengthen illegal trade and business, such as in arms and drugs, to gather foreign currency. 'If things get tough with legal trade because of sanctions, this country will move to illegal trade', says the European diplomat. 'It will flood the market with crystal meth, methamphetamine and other drugs; they can make a fortune if they move into the drug business.' Illegal gold smuggling and the arms trade also represent great opportunities, especially considering how costly and hard it is to maintain an efficient embargo. The diplomat continues:

> North Korea will find ways to go around the next round of sanctions. I think we have reached a level in which this country should be treated as equal and invited to sit at the table for negotiations with the others. I also think that the world has to accept that North Korea will become a nuclear power.

Rogue Nation Economics

It is likely that to offset the impact of the sanctions on the domestic economy, Kim Jong-un has been using the royal court economy. Kim Seung Chul, head of a North Korean defectors group in Seoul, has been analysing data referring to Kim Jong-un's usage of the royal court economy. Chul noticed a considerable fall in the number of presents the new leader is distributing. 'Records of Kim Jong-un's inspection tours show that he is expressing gratitude, this means a gift of words only.'[11] The occurrence of this type of gratitude 'present' increased in 2014 and remains very high.

Analysts like Chul also believe that the availability of foreign currency is becoming very tight, a fact that could explain why the new leadership has been using different strategies to gather foreign exchange. Among these is the export of the work of the Mansudae Art Studio, the company that made all the statues of the country's leaders in North Korea, including the famous bronze statues of Kim Il-sung and Kim Jong-il in Pyongyang in front of which North Koreans and foreigners are requested to pay their homages. The Mansudae Art Studio has been encouraged to export its skills abroad, for example, in Africa. In 2015 in Dakar, Senegal, the company completed a bronze statue of an African family that is higher than the Statue of Liberty and cost $25 million, half of which went to the North Korean regime. Sixty North Korean workers spent two years in Dakar to complete the work and were praised for their outstanding skills. Abdel Kader Fall at Senegal's Ministry of Culture said everybody was very happy about the project and the North Koreans went on to do similar projects in other African countries.[12] By the end of the year, North Korea had created more than thirty statues in Africa.

Exporting specialised labour abroad is also a way to bring foreign currency into North Korea. North Korean construction workers, for example, have been employed in Ulan Bator, the capital of Mongolia, earning $500 a month, and North Korean women have been employed in a sewing factory in Mongolia. According to the Mongolian employers, part of the salaries are delivered directly to Pyongyang. This is confirmed by the testimony of a North Korean construction worker interviewed by the *Washington Post*:

I worked for three and a half years [in St Petersburg], but I made only $2,000 during that time. We were allowed to work overseas for five years maximum, and I was hoping to save $10,000 and return home proud. I realized it wasn't going to happen, so I started looking for a chance to escape.[13]

North Korean labour has also been employed in several other industries, for example in the Siberian wood industry.[14]

In October 2017, the Saudi delegation participating in the UN-sponsored peace talks on Syria in Geneva accused North Korea of sending two militia units to fight alongside the Syrian army. No proof of such involvement has been provided, but this is not the first time that North Korean troops have been reported on Syrian soil. The US–Korea Institute has claimed that North Korean soldiers participated in the battle for Qusair in 2013.[15] Is Pyongyang also exporting soldiers in exchange for foreign exchange? It is possible.

Import data shows that in 2016, North Korean imports increased by $170 million over the previous year. This is a considerable jump during the imposition of sanctions. It is likely that remittances from workers employed abroad have been used to pay for imports. The US–Korea Institute estimates that the number of workers abroad is in the range of 50,000 people and that their individual annual incomes are about $10,000. In total they bring into the country $500 million in hard currency. This figure alone would be sufficient to cover two-thirds of the 2016 trade deficit.

The situation in 2017 may get much more serious. In February 2016 South Korea closed the Kaesong

Industrial Zone, which it is believed generated over $100 million annually earmarked for North Korean imports. But North Korea could compensate for such a loss by intensifying its bilateral trade with African countries and other nations. It is also making serious efforts to boost the tourism industry, even offering ski holidays in a new ski resort and allowing tourists to surf on its beaches.

North Korea is a beautiful country that has not been affected by mass tourism, something that can appeal to many people. This is part of the motivation that convinced Britain's fastest snowboarder, Jamie Barrow, and a group of snowboarders to visit the slopes of Masikryong in 2017. They were impressed by the beauty of the capital, where the buildings are painted in pastel colours, and by the large number of statues and monuments. Pyongyang has been constructed to celebrate the North Korean nation and to impress those who visit it. They saw large numbers of people rehearsing the traditional dance they would perform during the parades for the celebration for Kim Jong-un's birthday and from their hotel windows they watched the biggest fireworks display they had ever seen during these celebrations. After a four-hour ride they reached the ski resort, which seemed to pop out of nothing. The hotel was five star, with a swimming pool and even a hairdresser with a poster showing the regime's haircuts. The place was empty and so were the slopes. A treat for any skier who has battled huge lines at Western resorts. The day after, North Korean skiers came but, in comparison with Western resorts, their numbers were limited. The British snowboarders even taught their guides how to board.[16]

Marketisation of the Economy

Foreign trade remains a fundamental engine of growth. It also has a positive impact on internal markets, contributing to what Professor Byung-Yeon Kim describes as the marketisation of the North Korean economy. 'Today, about 70 to 80 per cent of household income comes from the market, which means that although North Korea is officially a socialist economy, it is in reality a marketised economy, i.e. market activities are very prevalent.'[17] Indeed, in 2016, 71.2 per cent of North Korean households participated in the informal economy and only 50.6 per cent of the total workforce was part of the official economy, that is, the state economy.[18]

The genesis of these dramatic changes is the collapse of the agricultural sector, discussed in Chapter 3. That crisis set the stage for a timid transition towards a market economy that has gained momentum over the years and has taken off since Kim Jong-un took power. In 2013, Kim Jong-un set out the *byungjin* line, a policy of simultaneous development of the nation's economy and nuclear program, permitting almost 400 markets with more than 600,000 stalls. These are in addition to countless unofficial markets, or *jangmadang,* technically illegal but tolerated, which constitute the backbone of the informal economy.[19]

It is worth analysing what has happened over the last four to six years in the rural areas, where the majority of people live. Agriculture is a sector that traditionally has been behind the industrial and urban areas. 'The difference between Pyongyang and the countryside is still huge, they are two different ball games altogether', explains the European diplomat I interviewed.

> The rural economy is still based on subsistence, i.e. there is very little saving and accumulation, but there has been an opening towards the market economy, for example, the regime tolerates that people barter and trade what they produce above their allocated quota.
>
> Over the last fifteen years European initiatives have supported user groups in the sloping lands, on average about ten families per group. If they use the sloping land according to principles of sustainable agroforestry, with reforestation for example, the groups get a land-use certificate from the Ministry of Land, Environment and Planning. This is a document which legally gives them the right to use the land.

Of course, this is not a private property title but something close to it that allows the groups to freely manage the land along agroforestry principles.

Because of these reforms, over the last four to six years there have been major changes in the way people relate to their work on the sloping land. 'Initially farmers would show me a lot of land where they grew potatoes and I would say "so you sell it on the market", they would immediately reply "no this is only for our own usage"', explains the European diplomat.

Today people talk about cash crops, they use a completely different language because they do sell or barter what they produce. They also have developed the concept of recognising market value chain. For example, those who produce maize on the sloping lands know how to increase the market value of their crop. They ask aid agencies to get them machinery to make noodles because they can mill the maize and if they can produce noodles, they can get a higher return on their crop.

In rural areas, the informal market economy is tolerated because this is the only way to avoid a crisis similar to what happened in the second half of the 1990s. According to the statistics published by Byung-Yeon Kim in his book *Unveiling the North Korean Economy: Collapse and Transition,* only 24.4 per cent of food is distributed through official channels, including food rationing and the state retail network.[20] However, some Western diplomats living in Pyongyang believe this figure is too low. Official statistics show that the state retail network, the Public Distribution System, still distributes an average 350 grams of cereals per person per day to those who don't work in the agriculture sector. The official figure would be 570 grams but this is never achieved – on the best days it reaches 420 grams. The marketisation of the agricultural sector is dictated by the need to guarantee food security to the entire nation, yet it also fits with the self-reliance ethos of the *juche* ideology.

As in the 1990s, people must find their own way to provide for themselves and for the market. The way the regime has introduced informal markets into an economy that is still officially socialist is by linking decentralisation with one of the imperatives of *juche*: be your own master. Indeed, North Koreans have proven to be very good at it.

'Through a very gradual process, agricultural cooperatives have been allowed to split into smaller units. A cooperative with 200 families becomes ten units with twenty families each. Whatever they produce above the quota is theirs. They can trade it and use the revenues as they please', says the European diplomat.

Some time ago I came across the manager of a tree nursery involved in the reforestation, he had invested the surplus money of the nursery to build a greenhouse to grow mushrooms. He basically started a business with mushrooms with and for the families that worked in the nursery. They grow and sell the mushrooms to their benefit. Profits may be reinvested in the business, to improve irrigation for example, or they can be divided among the families.

People use their initiative to transform their own gardens into cash crops, for instance by planting medicinal herbs. 'In the countryside, I have seen many households with up to twenty beehives in their small garden. We are not talking about proper plots of land but gardens that are not bigger than 100 to 150 square metres. The family trades or sells the honey to add value to the household economy.'

The informal economy is even more well established in urban areas, especially in Pyongyang. Unfortunately, this is also where one finds a much higher degree of corruption. 'Workers bribe their supervisor to leave the factory for most of the day to work in the informal economy, while still receiving a state salary', says the European diplomat. A North Korean dissident who escaped in 2014 confirms this analysis.

> I did so many things that I wasn't supposed to do. I worked as a broker transferring money and connecting people in North Korea with people in South Korea through phone calls. I arranged reunions for them in China. I smuggled antiques out of North Korea and sold them in China. I sold ginseng and pheasants to China. And I dealt ice [methamphetamine]. Officially, I was a factory worker, but I bribed my way out of having to go to work. If you don't operate this way in North Korea, you have nothing.[21]

As in the countryside, people have no choice, they must add ways and means to generate money because what they earn is insufficient. Here is how a North Korean doctor who escaped in 2014 described to the *Washington Post* his struggle to make ends meet.

> The salary for doctors was about 3,500 won a month. That was less than it cost to buy one kilogram of rice.

So of course, being a doctor was not my main job. My main job was smuggling at night. I would send herbal medicine from North Korea into China, and with the money, I would import home appliances back into North Korea. Rice cookers, notels, LCD monitors, that kind of thing.[22]

'On average, a family outside Pyongyang earns at least between 100 to 150 dollars or equivalent in goods and produce per month', the European diplomat goes on.

True, they have very little living costs: housing, electricity, heating, schooling, health care et cetera is provided for and free. However, food is expensive. I estimated that on average a family in the capital has a cash flow between 400 and 800 dollars per month. How did I get to this estimate? Well, I go to the supermarket and see how much food costs, but, recently, for example, I have noticed a big increase in the number of taxis in Pyongyang. There are about 2,000 that are run by state-owned taxi companies and they cost between 2 and 4 dollars a ride. People take them regularly, also to go to work, which means that they spend around 100 to 120 dollars per month in taxis alone. In urban areas, as in the countryside, the additional cash on top of state salaries comes from trading. 'Someone working in a shoe factory will have coupons to get shoes and their neighbour who works in a food factory has coupons for food, they trade their coupons', says the Chinese trader. This form of barter is well anchored to the value of the US dollar to which the local currency has an exchange rate of 8,000 won, reflecting the real value. 'A kilo of rice is 8,000 won so if someone trades a coupon for 3 kilograms of rice, he or she is basically saying that it is worth 3 dollars. If the shoe coupon has a different value, they trade something else to reach the exact monetary match or exchange dollars or euros.'

According to several diplomatic sources in Pyongyang, in the capital there is an increasingly large cash community. 'People have dollars and euros in their pockets', says another Western diplomat I interviewed in October 2017. 'I see it when they go to the supermarket, people pay also in dollars or euros.' As Evan Osnos writes in *The New Yorker*:

> North Koreans, outside their state-assigned jobs, sell homemade noodles in thriving markets; they drive private buses; they rent out apartments by the hour for courting couples...Kim has allowed limited economic reforms, letting people accumulate profits, which has fuelled the growth of black markets, including in real estate.[23]

How do North Koreans get foreign currency, especially when the country is the target of UN sanctions? 'The correct answer is through trade', explains the Chinese trader. 'For example, a state-holding institution, a fishery, sells 20 tonnes of fish to China, it gets paid in US dollars or RMB, pays its quota to the state and keeps the remaining amount of hard currency.' North Koreans are permitted to hold foreign currency, it is not prohibited as it was in the Soviet regime. 'I estimate that in the capital there is a cash economy worth about 100 million dollars, [this is] money in circulation either in dollar, euros or RMB', says the Western diplomat.

> The expatriate community, estimated to be approximately 500 to 1,000 foreigners, contributes around 2 million dollars per month through its expenditures for office operations, fuel, food and recreational activities. We cannot hold bank accounts and cannot pay in won, so we must buy everything in hard currency and in cash. Embassies and international institutions receive every month large cash deliveries to pay local salaries.

The experience of neighbouring China proves that opening the economy to the capitalist system is good for GDP but not for social cohesion. Clearly the DPRK regime wants to raise standards but needs to do it slowly. So it works on expectations, increasing them.

> Kim Jong-un promotes economic growth on his own terms. Every year since assuming power, he has unveiled a new residential complex in the capital, as well as theatres, a water park, and a new airport. This past spring, he attended the opening of more than three thousand new apartments on Ryomyong Street. [...] The green-and-white complex, which includes a seventy-story high-rise, has circular columns and bulging round balconies that give it a 'Jetsons'-like look.[24]

At the moment, the most serious internal dilemma that Kim Jong-un faces is how to maintain the status quo while allowing market forces into the economy.

Fun and Ordinary Life in North Korea

How to describe life in North Korea? 'Pyongyang is a cross between a kindergarten and a dance academy', says a Western-educated African businessman I interviewed in October 2017. But, as we saw in Chapter 3, it can also resemble the dystopian society of the *Divergent* trilogy.

Everything seems staged and, indeed, the regime is omnipresent in everyday life. 'People's lives are dictated by their *songbun*, i.e. the caste they belong to. Those at the lowest level, those born in the countryside, from a peasant's family, end up in the army for a decade, but they do not get to hold a weapon, they are not trained for combat, these people are de facto slave labourers for the system', explains the European diplomat.

These soldiers are not particularly bright, many carry the scars of malnutrition in childhood, for example they are very short. They are sent to the army after the compulsory schooling time, which is six to eight years, so they are eighteen, twenty years old. They perform the most difficult tasks, often living in very harsh conditions, such as sleeping in tents during the winter. They represent a huge asset for the regime practically at zero cost. During the floods in North Hamgyong in September 2016, the leadership brought 250,000 workers (soldiers) to reconstruct the entire area with 22,000 new housing units. When they told us diplomats that they would do it in two and a half months nobody believed it, but they did it.

The *songbun* and the exploitation of those belonging to the lowest caste seems to be the modern version of the chattel slavery that characterised the Koreas for millennia.

Another element of discrimination is beauty. 'There are so-called A, B and C girls in North Korea. The A girls are those you see at the airport, hotels, directing the traffic in Pyongyang, or wherever there are tourists. The regime scouts for good-looking girls and brings them to where they need them', says the European diplomat. 'The A girls also end up as soldiers marching in the parades. They only do that, they rehearse all year long and do not get trained in combat or fighting. The less good-looking girls are those who train as real soldiers.'

As in any totalitarian regime, people's lives are supervised from birth. In winter in Pyongyang it is common to see families taking children, as little as six months old, to nursery homes. The children go to school six days a week and are free on Sunday, this is when they spend time with their family. North Korean children are taught not to ask too many questions and are educated to accept the status quo, so they have a limited curiosity. So it is the school, that is, the state, that forges their mind. Many would describe this as brainwashing or ideological indoctrination.

'From an early age North Koreans are presented with a vision of their country [that] is totally idyllic', says a defector who resides in Canada. 'People have no reason to question it.' In winter, at intersections there are groups of women dressed in pink ski suits and red hats or other colourful dresses, holding huge red flags. The women dance and wave the flags, cheering people up in the morning hours.[25] People are brought up with the idea that the world outside the borders of North Korea is a dangerous place. To a certain extent, those living in Pyongyang resemble those living inside the Matrix. But, unlike the Matrix, North Koreans are not robots, as many are led to believe – they are real people.[26]

The lack of curiosity about the outside world springs from memories of the relentless bombing during the Korean War. These images are still very vivid; parents and grandparents as well as the propaganda of the regime keep them alive. The fear of those years has been transmitted to the younger generations. People cannot forget because of the military build-up of South Korea, the constant military exercises across the border, the presence of American troops in South Korea and the deployment of new weapons pointing at North Korea. Technically speaking, the two countries are still at war. Naturally, the regime uses the politics of fear to its own advantage, stressing the fundamental role that the leadership plays in protecting the nation and the people from the enemy across the southern border and across the Pacific Ocean. North Koreans live inside this propaganda cocoon, which makes them feel secure. Are they happy? In the way that ignorance is bliss, yes, they seem satisfied with what they have at home.[27]

Foreigners who have lived in North Korea concur that North Koreans not only are not used to asking questions, they also have a limited time to reflect on and think about politics. The regime organises their life from birth to death, filling it up with communal tasks that keep people busy all the time. 'At the end of the day people are too tired to discuss politics, all they want to do is to rest and relax with their family', says the European diplomat. According to the 2017 Human Rights Watch report on North Korea, 'All North Korean families also have to send one family member for at least two hours per day, six days a week, to support local government construction or public beautification projects, like building structures, fixing roads, collecting raw materials like crushed stone, or cleaning public areas'.[28]

All North Koreans are part of units or groups related to what they do and where they live, so there are youth units, work units, rural units, neighbourhood units and so on. The neighbourhood units range from twenty to forty families living in the same building or street. They are generally run by someone who is old and has a good social status, (*songbun*), and, of course, is a member of the party. 'The units have specific tasks', explains the European diplomat.

> I remember that when I was living in Pyongyang I used to see women mending the flower beds along the road, cleaning the streets, in winter they removed the snow. Men do other tasks, for example they resurface the roads. Basically, people do not pay taxes but they contribute to society or the state performing these tasks. Twice a year the entire population is mobilised

for rice planting and harvesting. Everybody goes, including members of the elite. The idea behind it can be summarised by the North Korean motto: the one who eats rice must plant rice.

Defectors describe these tasks as compulsory and harsh.

[Their] schools forced them to work for free on farms twice a year, for one month at a time, during ploughing and seeding time, and again at harvest time. A former school teacher who escaped North Korea in 2014 said his school forced its students (aged between 10 and 16) to work every day to generate funds to pay government officials, maintain the school, and make a profit.[29]

In the countryside the units are less regimented than in the city. The famine of the late 1990s has softened the control exercised through the units. The regime understands that people cannot perform these tasks while they cannot feed themselves. In rural areas, in particular, people need a higher degree of mobility to find food. In the post-famine era, those in charge of units are not impervious to bribery. This is also true in urban areas. As discussed in the previous chapters, corruption is widespread in North Korea and to a certain extent it is tolerated and even softens the feudal justice system. There is no doubt that bribes offer a safety valve against the rigidity of the system, not only at an economic but also at a social level.

Wealth is clearly another element of discrimination among North Koreans. 'Wealth can get you access to a better life, you can buy your way up the social ladder', says the European diplomat. The timid liberalisation has produced an entrepreneurial elite known as *donju,* masters of money. This elite, made up of government insiders, imports housewares, medicine and luxury products from China.[30] Kim Jong-un knows about it and so far has allowed members of *donju* to accumulate profits, which has fuelled the growth of informal markets, because it helps reduce the impact of the sanctions.

The family-nation background of the regime was used to create a strong value system based on traditional Korean moral principles and it is down this social path that the majority of people's lives evolve, always under the supervision of the leadership. 'They are like children, they never fully grow up. The regime makes all the important decisions for them. As in school, the most diligent citizens are rewarded and this is a source of great pride while, at the same time, it reinforces the value system', explains a North Korean defector I interviewed who resides in the UK.

The story of Mun Gan sun, a textile factory worker in Pyongyang, is the typical modern-day North Korean fairytale. An orphan, she was looked after by the state. After completing a basic education, she moved to the capital where she became a model factory worker, producing even four times as much as the other workers. When the local TV station filmed an official visit of Kim Jong-il to the factory she worked at, Mun Gan sun was praised for her work. A student at the technological university in Pyongyang saw the program and decided that for him she would be the ideal wife. So he asked to meet her. They married and now have one child. The couple lives in a beautiful two-bedroom flat in the capital, which was given to Mun Gan sun in appreciation for her hard work. From her kitchen balcony she can see the big bronze statue of Kim Il-sung and the family starts every day bowing to that statue. In 2012 Kim Jong-un visited the building, thanking Mun Gan sun personally. A big picture from his visit hangs in her living room.[31]

Dating can be problematic in North Korea because the society is extremely conservative. On university campuses, for example, dating is forbidden. However, young people do find a way to go on dates outside the campus. They meet in restaurants, they go on hikes together, they organise picnics on the riverbank and at the beach. In an interview with *The Independent,* Jummin Kang, a North Korean defector, admits that he was able to spend hours with his girlfriend while he was a teenager in Pyongyang. During the week they went on walks along the river and on weekends they went to the cinema. Intimacy, however, is very limited. 'You can't kiss in public places[;] it's not illegal, but it's not a cultural practice', he recalls. 'You're also not supposed to have sex before you are married.'[32] However, when it comes to sex, even young North Koreans break the rules. 'Parents are often at work all day so couples will go to their house. When I was young I saw a couple having sex in the park', says Kang. Young people also meet in social clubs. During the holidays, these clubs host large dances and parties, the most famous ones being those held in Kim Il-sung square in Pyongyang.

Homosexuality is a huge taboo to the extent that young people do not even know exactly what it is. 'It was very tough for me', remembers a North Korean homosexual who escaped to South Korea via China as soon as he finished high school.

> I did not understand what was happening to me, I could not talk to anybody. North Korea is the kind of society where digressing from 'normality' is a crime and a sin at the same time. When I was sent to the countryside to work[,] the atmosphere got less tense, there was more freedom, less control. In one of these trips I met a couple of other homosexual people. It was a great comfort for all of us to know that we were not freaks. We planned to run away together. I did not even say goodbye to my parents, if they had known that I was gay they would have been deeply ashamed.[33]

While in school, teenagers are sent every year for a fortnight to work in the countryside. Farming is a hard-working experience, but many youngsters enjoy the freedom of these two weeks. Because the regime does not exercise the same control in the countryside that it does in urban areas, (especially in Pyongyang, which is regarded as the flagship of the nation's ethics and morality), in rural areas students party every night outdoors and meet members of the opposite sex.

Koreans love to party. They even have a specific word for it: *eumjugamu,* which literally means music, dance and drink. *Eumjugamu* can be traced back to the shamanic tradition and the ancient Korean festivals, so it is deeply rooted in the entertainment culture of both South and North Koreans. Partying means drinking beer and *soju* (a colourless spirit traditionally based on potatoes or rice), often followed by an hour or two in a *noraebang* (karaoke bar). There is no shortage of alcoholic drinks in North Korea. In recent times, a private trade in alcohol has emerged, together with a number of microbreweries in urban areas. Mass market beer, however, is cheap and available, as is *soju*, which remains the most cost-effective and legal way of getting drunk. In the countryside North Koreans produce homemade moonshine, or *nongtaegi,* and they brew their own beer. They ferment whatever they have: corn, fruit or ginseng. House parties are also very common. Instead of karaoke, people use an instrument and sing along.

At home a few people watch South Korean soaps and movies. Though prohibited, the DVDs can be bought in the informal markets.

Kim Jong-un recently launched a North Korean Netflix-style service called Manbang that enables people to re-watch documentaries about their leaders as well as to learn Russian and English languages. Manbang supposedly offers five channels that show state-sanctioned news and educational programs.[34]

Some teenagers also video chat on their smartphones. North Korea 'develops its own smartphones, which connect to the national intranet, meaning users can access (North Korean) websites and apps. Granted, the vast majority of North Koreans can't afford this.'[35] Western diplomats estimate that there are 3.5 million mobile phones in North Korea, of which about 20 per cent are smartphones. This number is too large for phone ownership to be considered the sole domain of 'an elite social class'. Dissidents seem to disagree, however, stressing that only rich people can afford smartphones.[36]

Kim Jong-un has created several amusement parks where people can enjoy the outdoors. In 2012 he opened the Rungra People's Pleasure Ground together with his wife, Ri Sol-ju. The Kaeson Youth Park covers more than 400,000 square metres, while Munsu Water Park features about twenty-six pools for families to swim in and enjoy. For $8 people can horseback ride in the Mirim Riding Club. There are also ice-skating rinks, a zoo and a circus. Since Kim Jong-un came to power, people have often been taken to these parks as a reward by the institution they work for, whether a state department, ministry or a factory.

Those who cannot afford the entry ticket for these parks can relax by fishing in the river, swimming at the beaches or hiking in the hills and mountains.

Chapter 5

Cyber Scapegoat

North Korea is regularly blamed for the most spectacular cybercrimes committed in the global village. Generally, after major cyberattacks, accusations against Pyongyang circulate, get picked up and consolidated by the media until eventually they are viewed as facts. In part this is due to attribution of a state actor in cybercrime being 'very, very difficult', says cybersecurity and threat assessment expert Jeremy Samide, who I interviewed in September 2017. One could add that attribution is hard in general, to the extent that 'Pinning a cybercrime to a cybercriminal is a Sisyphean task'.[1] Yet the international cybersecurity community has a clear idea of the capabilities of state actors and agrees that North Korea has a much smaller cyber footprint than Russia, China, the United Kingdom or the United States. These are the true cyber giants, as Edward Snowden has revealed.

North Korea also lacks the required skills because the bulk of the population does not have access to the internet, therefore it doesn't have a natural pool of talent to recruit from. In addition, the sanctions limit its exposure to new technology.[2] Reports of large buildings in Pyongyang or of luxury hotels in China where an army of North Korean hackers work 24/7 and regularly break into world corporations, banks and national security agencies using the most up-to-date cyber tools are fantasies; they belong to the propaganda that surrounds North Korea, the nation we love to hate.

What the international cybersecurity community will say, however, is that North Korea does have the capability to commit major crimes. It is not a cyber giant but nor is it a dwarf. As do China, Russia, the USA, the UK and other governments, the North Korean leadership recognises the importance of cyberwarfare and has been investing in this sector, diligently practising cyberespionage. According to South Korea's National Intelligence Service, the new leadership has given fresh impetus to cyberwarfare, with Kim Jong-un more than once describing it as strategically important to Pyongyang as missiles and nuclear weapons.[3]

Bureau 121

According to Kim Heung-kwang, a defector who trained many North Korean hackers, in the early 1990s Kim Jong-il decided to invest in cyberwarfare, imitating China. About fifteen North Koreans were selected for their outstanding maths skills and sent to a military academy in China to be trained. When they returned, they became the core of a new unit, External Information Intelligence Office (EIIO), whose task was to hack into websites, penetrate firewalls and steal information abroad. They used China as a bridge to reach the cyber universe because access to the internet in North Korea was and still is extremely limited. Kim Il-sung saw the net as a danger for the nation, an avenue of Westernisation and corruption of values, so the DPRK has its own intranet.[4]

Eventually Bureau 121 was created, a de facto cyber-attack unit, part of the Reconnaissance General Bureau, North Korea's primary intelligence agency.[5] Reports about Bureau 121 are contradictory: some defectors claim there are about 1,800 hackers[6] and others say there are over 6,000.[7] In any case, this is much fewer than those working for the United States or Russia, or Google. Western diplomats who have lived in North Korea as well as the international cybersecurity community warn about what defectors say.

> Much of what is reported about North Korea's cyber army comes from defectors or rival governments with a spin motive and is amplified by partisan or attention-seeking media. Defectors' insights are valuable, yes. But even if they're not politically motivated, they are limited by the scope of their access and inside knowledge – and are usually significantly out of date.[8]

Yet everybody concurs that those working for Bureau 121 represent an elite force. They are all handpicked from the prestigious University of Automation, North Korea's military college for computer science, after a five-year course. The regime treats them and their family very well, says Jang Se-yul, who studied at the University of Automation before defecting to South Korea, providing them with good housing facilities and other special privileges.[9]

These types of reward are necessarily rare because they follow exceptional performances, such as hacking for the DPRK. Indeed, the regime's propaganda has been presenting cyberwarfare as an effective, essential and relatively inexpensive form of national defence; a handful of hackers can damage the infrastructure of an enemy, and for a country like North Korea this is a vital advantage. Hacking can also be a source of income, for example, using ransomware.[10] So far the media has reported that North Korea's main target has been South Korea, as shown by several major cyberattacks.

In 2013, on the anniversary of the outbreak of the Korean War, South Korea was hit by multiple cyber-attacks launched by hackers identified as the DarkSeoul gang. They targeted a number of official websites, including the presidential Blue House.[11] It soon became clear that the same hackers had hit South Korea before, in March that year, when they masterminded the devastating Jokra cyberattacks, and in May, when they carried out cyberattacks against South Korean financial companies.[12] Many believe that the Jokra attacks were a mix of intimidation and robbery. The hackers did not disguise the malware, as if they wanted to send a specific, clear message to Seoul: that Pyongyang could reach into the heart of South Korea's economy without blowing up warships or shelling any city. Indeed, the attacks paralysed parts of the country. The computers of South Korea's two leading television stations, the Korean Broadcasting System and MBC, and of YTN, the cable channel, were all frozen.[13] Though no evidence has been provided by the companies themselves – no bank would admit to having been robbed by hackers if it can avoid it – it is likely that the hackers were also able to steal money. They hit the internet banking of Shinhan Bank, the country's fourth-largest lender, and infected the computer system of NongHyup, Jeju and Woori banks with viruses.[14]

Several cybersecurity experts agreed that North Korea may have the cyber capacity but it has a limited reach, for example, the country is not linked to submarine cables and depends on China's servers, its actions are geographically limited and most likely monitored by Beijing. However, 'because attribution is very difficult it is relatively easy to make it look like a cyberattack coming from North Korea', explains Jeremy Samide. 'In the digital world we live in, it is sufficient to leave artefacts, evidence, tactical procedures, digital prints and other targeted clues pointing at the DPRK.'

Because law enforcement, governments and states very rarely manage to conclusively attribute responsibility for a big cybercrime, especially when a state sponsor is involved, pointing the finger at a rogue nation like North Korea provides an answer that the community easily accepts. Blaming North Korea, the cyber scapegoat, also reduces the pressure on law enforcement to answer uncomfortable questions about how secure our electronic data is. Finally, psychologically, people are keener to accept that they have been the victim of a rogue state than of a group of hackers still at large in cyberspace. It's even more uncomfortable to admit that a major cybercrime was an inside job, as proven by how the media, law enforcement and Sony itself handled the Sony hacking incident – one of the biggest in modern history.

Hacking Hollywood

On 22 November 2014 the computer screens of Sony's employees began showing skulls and a message threatening to expose 'secrets' from data that hackers had stolen. Sony reacted, as any corporation or bank would, by attempting to sort out the mess in-house. 'In many circumstances, if the news of the cyberattack has not become public and has not been posted on the internet, corporations will try to keep a lid on it while they attempt to fix the problem', explains Jeremy Samide. But the news of the Sony hacking did go public and became a sensational news story because it involved emails, pictures, films and data of Hollywood stars.

North Korea was blamed for two main reasons. The code used to perpetrate the attack, called Destover, was similar to the one that investigators believed North Korea had used in the past to hack South Korea, though the code had been in circulation around the world for quite a while. Confirmation of the involvement of the DPRK seemed to come when the hackers, who identified them-selves as the Guardians of Peace, demanded that Sony cancel the release of *The Interview*, a satire about the assassination of Kim Jong-un.[15] This news was a golden opportunity for Guardians of Peace to cover their tracks and divert the investigation towards a state sponsor – North Korea. It was also a golden opportunity for Sony to get publicity for a film that was about to be released.

Sony latched on to the story and used it to counteract the negative response of the critics, many of whom had predicted that *The Interview* was going to be a big flop. After declaring that it would not release it, Sony decided to show the film in a limited number of cinemas on Christmas Day. Even with the hype created by the hacking, the revenues generated were a modest $12–15 million, which just covered the cost of production.[16]

To date, no proof of North Korean involvement in the Sony hacking has been produced, but there is plenty of speculation about the insufficient evidence of its involvement. Several cyber experts have expressed the opinion that in the hacking of Sony, as in the Bangladesh Bank's cyberheist discussed in the following section, there were indications of one or more insiders. An unnamed Sony executive had confirmed to *TMZ* magazine that insiders, who knew where the most embarrassing information could be found, had helped the hackers.[17] *TMZ*'s source explained that it would have been very difficult for an outsider to find such information. The hackers knew the mail system and its configuration, they also knew the internal IT system, including how the payroll worked. Finally, *TMZ* claims that 'several people suggested a possible link between the hackers and Sony layoffs, which included a large number of IT employees'.[18] And Sony employees within IT were well read on destructive malware and its capabilities. In 2005 and 2007, Sony put a version of malware on its CDs so that if people copied or shared them, it would destroy the user's hard drive.[19] Indeed, some cyber investigators believe that former employees were able to join forces with the hacker community, who had long resented Sony's anti-piracy stance.[20]

Another controversial aspect is why, if North Korea was involved, it did not cash in on the hacking. The hackers had access to the passwords of Sony's financial accounts. With the documents they stole, they could have done several things to make money, from theft to sale of intellectual property to extortion. But they did not, they simply released the files on the internet in an attempt to humiliate the entertainment giant.[21]

Lazarus

Regardless of the involvement of state actors, the key question is how vulnerable we all are in cyberspace, a new and expanding dimension of our life. The investigation into the 2017 WannaCry ransomware attack,[22] the biggest in history, exposed our profound vulnerability to cybercrime. It also unveiled interesting facts that seem to confirm that North Korea is a convenient scapegoat for the weakness of the cybersecurity systems that are meant to protect us.

Investigators went back more than a decade to identify the hackers who masterminded WannaCry. They discovered that behind every attack attributed to North Korea was the same sophisticated villain, a group of hackers known as Lazarus, who may have created a virtual malware factory that could launch more powerful attacks in the future. The group may use digital or real secret lairs in Northeast China, from where North Korea cyber activity has been conducted. Lazarus appears to be a cyber mercenary battalion, motivated by profit, but also sensitive to political and financial issues as it picks and chooses its clients and targets. The consensus is that Lazarus was behind the WannaCry incident.[23]

One of the main features of the dark net is the cooperation and an esprit de corps among those who operate inside it. 'There is a culture of information sharing, acceptance for the elite and a professional courtesy among the hacking community, of looking out for each other', says Jeremy Samide.

At times misunderstood and almost always hidden in plain sight, many of them collaborate on activities for what they perceive to be the greater good of our society. Malware is one of the many byproducts of this culture. It is a global issue with exponential proliferation and it is constantly transforming into different mutations, something that comes out today may be different tomorrow, but with the same DNA. They [the hackers] are always modifying it, making it better in order to circumvent the latest security technologies.

Moreover, the hacking community constantly improves its tools, techniques and strategies, which are shared almost in real time, and the outcome is a constant mutation of malware. To a certain extent, conceptually, the sharing culture of the hacking community is not very different from that of the birth of Bitcoin or even the self-reliance ideology of *juche*. These are closed communities that have erected huge walls around themselves, modern sects where the members trust and protect each other and are so integrated that they act almost as a single entity. So the theory of Lazarus being a collective does make sense.

Cooperation is not a main characteristic of national cybersecurity or of state sponsors of cybercrimes. 'States will cooperate only up to a certain level and when it is convenient', explains Samide, and this cooperation can be very limited. Governments would never exchange vital and classified information. Because of that, the asymmetry between cybercrime and cyberwarfare attackers and their targets may not be as big as it is presented. States are stronger and governments have deep pockets, but they lack one of the fundamental tools to develop effective cyberdefence and attack mechanisms: they do not trust each other. In the absence of a proper weapon they blame the DPRK.

In 2016, cyber analytics company Novetta led an independent industry investigation of the Sony hacking, known as Operation Blockbuster, and came to the conclusion that Lazarus was responsible. The report says the attack 'was carried out by a single group, or potentially very closely linked groups, sharing technical resources, infrastructure and even tasking'.[24] Lazarus's fingerprints were also found on 2007 and 2009 hackings in the USA and in South Korea. Operation Blockbuster even linked Lazarus to the DarkSeoul attack in 2013 and ruled out that Lazarus is part of North Korea's cyber warriors, finding no proof of any link with the DPRK. Even more surprising, according to James Scott, a senior fellow at the Institute for Critical Infrastructure Technology, a Washington-based think tank, is that no conclusive evidence exists that Lazarus is state-sponsored exists. Lazarus has 'always exhibited the characteristics of a well-resourced and organized cybercriminal or cyber-mercenary collective'.[25] Interestingly the USA has not blamed WannaCry on North Korea.

The Dark Net

If in 2018 the economic sanctions begin to bite, as many believe they will, the best service that North Korean hackers may perform for their country is to offer access to the dark net to conduct illegal activities. The European diplomat I interviewed who resided in Pyongyang for four years is convinced that the regime will not hesitate to get into illegal activities, from production and sale of illicit drugs to the sale of counterfeit currency. Trade in crystal meth or methamphetamine, for example, is worth several billion dollars. It is easy to produce and at the moment the biggest producer is situated in Myanmar, but a state actor like North Korea could easily rival such output. All these illicit businesses and activities can be conducted through the dark net using cryptocurrencies like Bitcoin, Ethereum and Litecoin.

Jeremy Samide concurs that the DPRK has the capability to make money through cybercrime, from coordinating sophisticated phishing campaigns in buying and selling stolen personally identifiable information, intellectual property and proprietary data, to money laundering in cryptocurrencies. North Korea is already ensconsed in cryptocurrencies and there have been several reports that it uses this digital cash to circumvent the sanctions, for example, by clearing import-export activities, such as selling arms and buying oil from Iran or Libya. 'Cryptocurrencies support a huge economy and distribution of a variety of goods and services at the moment', confirms Samide.

> These anonymous currencies make it easier to buy weapons, drugs and any other illicit goods and services without using cash. Indeed, this economy has been growing at a phenomenal rate because crypto-currencies are becoming more widely accepted. It is a system based on trust, which is not so different from the international monetary system.

Most likely, Pyongyang is already involved in money laundering using cryptocurrencies. The mechanism is relatively simple. Someone is infected with ransomware and ultimately pays a ransom in Bitcoin, which at some point needs to be exchanged for cash. The challenge is how to do it without leaving a sizeable footprint.

Exchanging small amounts, one or two bitcoins for example, is not easily detected, but larger sums can be easy to trace and can stand out in the blockchain ledger.[26] So people use unregulated cryptocurrency exchanges. They are all over the world and North Korea could get into this business – it has the capability to do so.

Autopsy of the Cyberheist of the Bangladesh Bank

On Thursday 4 February 2016, the Federal Reserve Bank of New York received a series of payment orders via SWIFT, the interbank communication system, from the Bangladesh Bank for a total of $951 million. The first order arrived in New York just after 9.55 am, which was 7.55 pm in Dhaka. It amounted to $20 million payable to the account of a charity in Sri Lanka, Shalika. The following thirty-four orders reached New York over the next four hours.

On a daily basis, the Federal Reserve Bank of New York handles about $800 billion, so the request to transfer $1 billion did not generate any suspicion about a possible cyberheist. However, the Bangladesh Bank had never moved such large sums of money or asked for so many transfers at once; in the previous twelve months it had averaged as little as two transfer orders per day. The account holders on the orders were all individuals and not institutions, which was also odd for a central bank. Finally, the thirty-five orders lacked the names of the corresponding banks, the banks through which the payment from the Federal Reserve Bank of New York would reach the banks of the recipient accounts. This was a major irregularity that blocked all the SWIFT orders.[27]

The Federal Reserve sent a message to the Bangladesh Bank asking to fix the documentation, which the hackers intercepted and answered. When the message was sent it was the middle of the night in Bangladesh, however, the orders came back right away with the correct formatting. Nobody in New York wondered how they got such a prompt reply from a bank that was closed. The Federal Reserve began processing the orders. Five went through automatically because they were properly SWIFT authenticated.

What stopped the remaining thirty payments and triggered a proper investigation was the name of one of the recipient accounts, Jupiter, which happened to be the same name as an oil tanker and oil shipping company under the United States' sanctions program against Iran. Overall, it took twelve hours to realise that something was wrong and to alert the Bangladesh Bank. By then it was Friday morning in Bangladesh, the first day of the weekend.[28] The Bangladesh Bank was closed but a few staff were working. Yet they never received any message from New York because the hackers had sabotaged the communication system of the bank. In New York, a day after the arrival of the orders from Bangladesh, the Federal Reserve began a manual review because no reply had arrived from Dhaka.

In the meantime, the first five transfers, worth $101 million, had already been executed. Luckily, one of them, the $20 million transfer to Sri Lanka, was blocked by the corresponding bank because of a typo in the documentation. But $81 million did go through and was transferred to four accounts in the Philippines. From there the money was quickly moved and laundered inside Southeast Asia's casino industry. When the Federal Reserve attempted to reverse the transfers, the $81 million had already vanished.

It was soon uncovered that the Bangladesh Bank had been hit by a very cleverly orchestrated cyberheist. The hackers had an in-depth knowledge of how the international banking system worked and therefore could exploit its shortcomings, both in Bangladesh and in New York. They knew that, 'while credit card companies can spot unusual patterns in real time, the New York Fed typically looks back through payments, usually the day after they are requested'.[29] It was a 'total fluke' that the New York Federal Reserve did not pay out all $951 million.

The Bangladesh Bank cyberheist was the first of many similar high-profile, cyber-focused robberies. It set the mould for a new paradigm where targeted computer hacking coupled with malicious banking malware is combined with traditional money-laundering techniques. To date, nobody knows how the hackers gained access to the SWIFT transfer money network, until then considered extemely secure. It was an out-standing cybercrime operation and, because of that, it was blamed on the DPRK, which, of course, was not true.

It turned out that the four days after the robbery were crucial for the investigation. 'The bank itself did not organise any outside investigation right away, that is generally the window of time, soon after you have been compromised, when you have the highest level of ability to go in and get some clear data about what happened and who was behind it', explains Laura Galante, a cybersecurity expert I interviewed who worked for the US company that investigated the Bangladesh Bank's cyberheist.

> Because that window was relatively closed by the time the investigators were on the scene, what had happened was very confusing. For example, what has never been clear are the motives and tools used. Because there was so much conflicting data about motives and tools, a lot of theories began emerging.

Cybersecurity and threat assessment expert Jeremy Samide adds,

> These are some of the toughest and most trivial components to an investigation: the tactics, techniques and procedures used by the bad actors. You need to not only answer the 'what', but the 'how' and the 'why' are as equally important to understand the bigger picture.

Another important element to consider is that the cyberheist triggered a panic inside the international banking system. Not because of the large sums of money stolen, but because the hackers had penetrated the SWIFT system. 'Nobody had ever used the SWIFT credential of employees in a cyberheist; this really struck fear in everybody. It was because of that that the idea of state sponsors began taking shape', Galante continues. The banking community wanted to stress that a group of criminals could not have committed the cyberheist, it required exceptional capabilities that bank robbers do not have, so it had to be a state-sponsored operation.

'It is common in these situations that North Korea gets blamed', Galante says, even if experts know that the DPRK does not have the infrastructure to carry out as sophisticated a cyber robbery as the Bangladesh Bank heist. Until October 2017, North Korea's main connection to the international internet was through a fibre-optic cable that connects Pyongyang with Dandong, in China, and crosses the border at Sinuiju. The internet access was provided by China Unicom and since the end of 2017 the DPRK has also had access to a Russian server.[30] More important is the fact that 'North Korea does not have submarine cables', says Nirjhar Mazumder, a Bangladeshi journalist and blogger who is in hiding in Europe because of death threats from jihadists. 'How could it have masterminded the Bangladesh Bank's cyberheist without them?'[31]

Nevertheless, in May 2016, Bloomberg reported the allegation that North Korea was behind the cyber robbery. The article used as a reference two anonymous sources related to World Informatix Cyber Security, the organisation that the Bangladesh Bank appointed to investigate the heist.[32] The media continues to refer to the heist as a North Korean cybercrime even if, to date, no solid proof of the DPRK being involved has been produced. On the contrary, there are plenty of official reports and investigations that affirm that the robbery was most likely an inside job and that North Korea was not involved at all. Blaming the DPRK has proven very convenient for the institutions involved, including the Bangladesh Bank, as it somehow makes them look more like victims than incompetent organisations.

On 17 March 2016, Tanvir Hassan Zoha, a Bangladeshi cybersecurity expert who was working on the investigation into the heist, went missing. Days before the abduction, in an interview with *Bangla Tribune*, he opined that the heist could not have been done without the involvement of an insider. Zoha was found six days after his abduction.[33]

'Zoha was an ICT expert who helped various law enforcement agencies with technical support', explains Mazumder. 'After the heist, the Rapid Action Battalion, an elite law enforcement agency, started a shadow investigation and appointed Zoha to help them, though unofficially.' In a rare interview conducted by Mazumder after Zoha's release, Zoha elaborated on his task in the investigation. 'My primary work was to find out if the system had been infected remotely or if it had been done deliberately by someone.'[34]

The Criminal Investigation Department (CID) of the Bangladesh police did detect negligence on the part of at least thirteen officials of four departments of the Bangladesh Bank. CID's additional inspector general Shah Alam said, 'We have also identified 25 citizens of the Philippines, Sri Lanka, and China who were involved in this major bank heist'.[35]

'Based on the evidence, facts and other elements that I saw during my short involvement in the investigation, there is simply a lack of evidence of North Korea's involvement', admitted Zoha. 'We lack concrete proof or any definite clue through which we can point at North Korea, that I can say.'[36] Laura Galante is also sceptical about the involvement of North Korea. 'North Korea is not the biggest and most efficient state sponsor of cybercrime in the world. Not at all. But it often gets blamed. People see asymmetrical capabilities and because North Korea is willing to cross these lines, they assume that it has the capabilities to carry on huge attacks.' Jeremy Samide expands on this point:

> With very little pushback or rebuttal of these global accusations, this bodes well for the DPRK from an intelligence and counterintelligence perspective. This fuels the already brazen leader and amplifies the propaganda machine in favour of a much stronger, more organised and highly cyberskilled North Korea. In many ways, these accusations embolden the country's posture in being viewed as a top-tier, global adversary.

Chapter 6

The Last Evil Standing

In December 1975, A. Q. Khan, a young Pakistani scientist working for Urenco, a consortium of European governments that operates a top-secret uranium enrichment facility in the Netherlands, boarded a plane with his South African wife and flew to Pakistan for the Christmas holidays. He never returned.

In his briefcase Khan was carrying the top-secret blueprints of a new technology to arm a nuclear bomb, documents he had stolen from his employer that he would use to fulfil his dream: to provide Pakistan with a nuclear device to counter India's newly manufactured atomic weapon. Yet, over time, Khan's motivations became less patriotic and he sold nuclear technology to other countries in exchange for large sums of money.

For more than a quarter of a century, A. Q. Khan built and ran the world's largest clandestine network of nuclear secrets, an atomic bazaar, with the backing of various Pakistani governments and generals. In their book *Deception*, investigative journalists Adrian Levy and Catherine Scott-Clark reveal that US, British and other intelligence services knew a great deal about him and his business. They could have shut it down long before Khan provided nuclear technology to Iran, Libya, North Korea and possibly to other state and non-state actors. But they did not. Successive US administrations, from Jimmy Carter to George W. Bush, turned a blind eye to Khan's network in return for favours from Pakistan, first in funnelling arms to the mujaheddin during the anti-Soviet jihad in Afghanistan and, after 9/11, in helping with the global war on terror. Ironically, failing to act against Khan and his Pakistani backers facilitated the spread of the very weapons of mass destruction upon which, according to Bush, the Axis of Evil took shape.[1]

The Axis of Evil

In 2002, during his State of the Union address, George W. Bush described Iraq, Iran and North Korea as the Axis of Evil, a group of nations that put peace in the world at risk. These countries, he claimed, had violated international law by securing arms of mass destruction and by preventing the entry of UN inspectors whose task was to verify that civil nuclear energy programs were not destined for military scope. In addition, all these countries were governed by dictatorial regimes that opposed the West and would not hesitate to ally themselves with its enemies, including terrorists.

In the aftermath of 9/11, it was easy for President Bush to project an apocalyptic nuclear scenario in order to convince people that one or more members of the Axis of Evil could and would help a terrorist organisation get hold of nuclear warheads. This certainly struck the fear of God in America and in the rest of the world. After 9/11, the image of a mushroom cloud rising above New York City's skyline didn't seem surreal.

Because emotions were running high, in 2002 very few people in power saw any contradictions in Bush's nightmarish theory. Yet no proof that Iraq had weapons of mass destruction or that there were links between Saddam Hussein and Osama bin Laden was ever produced. Today we know that the Bush and Blair administrations manufactured false evidence to lure the world into a preventive strike in Iraq. People and the media also seemed to ignore the absence from the Axis of Evil of Pakistan, a nuclear country that had been bankrolling the Taliban, al Qaeda's hosts, and had been selling nuclear secrets for more than two decades.

The Bush administration kept very quiet about the role Pakistan had played in the development of the nuclear programs of the countries in the Axis of Evil. It also never revealed that American intelligence had proof that A. Q. Khan had visited North Korea several times.[2] Since 9/11, Pakistan had ceased to be part of the rogue nations secretly developing the nuclear bomb and had become a valuable ally in the war on terror. Just two weeks after 9/11, seeking support for the invasion of Afghanistan, Bush ended the sanctions the USA had imposed on Pakistan following the completion of its nuclear weapons program.

Those who knew what the Bush administration had in mind – using the war on terror to strike Iraq and bring about a regime change – thought that the inclusion of North Korea in the Axis of Evil was a cover-up. John Feffer, author of *North Korea, South Korea: US Policy at a Time of Crisis*, adds that it made the war on terror look less like a Christian crusade against Muslims and more like a clash between good and evil, a sort of remake of the Cold War dichotomy when America was the good guy and the USSR the villain. Like Iraq, North Korea was ruled by a dictator and Bush stressed the need to remove Saddam Hussein. The DPRK was also a country with a nuclear program and sufficiently unknown to be described as evil. The word 'evil' was fundamental. It had been purposely chosen to rule out any diplomatic effort, famously summarised by Dick Cheney: 'You do not negotiate with evil. You destroy evil.'[3]

As the goal of creating the Axis of Evil was to engender a regime change in Iraq, Washington had no plan to invade North Korea or to remove Kim Jong-il, who for another decade continued to do business with Pakistan.

The Islamabad–Pyongyang Axis

In February 2004, under mounting pressure from President Musharraf, A. Q. Khan publicly confessed to having supplied nuclear technology and components to North Korea, Iran and Libya. During the telecast, he denied that the Pakistani government or the military had been involved in this business. Which, of course, was a lie.

According to Benazir Bhutto, army chief general Mirza Aslam Beg was the driving force behind the idea of proliferation for monetary gain.[4] In 2011, the *Washington Post* reported that Khan had released proof that in 1998 the DPRK had transferred $3 million to former Pakistani army chief Jehangir Karamat and half a million dollars and some jewellery to another military official.[5] Clearly Khan was the salesman and Pakistan was the owner of the atomic bazaar. Intelligence officials reported that he 'sold North Korea much of the material needed to build a bomb, including high-speed centrifuges used to enrich uranium and the equipment required to manufacture more of them'.[6]

The Islamabad–Pyongyang nuclear business exchanges started during Pakistani Prime Minister Zulfikar Ali Bhutto's visit to North Korea in 1976.[7] North Korea had begun its nuclear adventure in the late 1950s in response to the American nuclear build-up in South Korea. The USSR had agreed to set up its first plutonium-based nuclear reactor at Yongbyon-Kun for peaceful use of nuclear technology. However, in the mid-1970s what Kim Il-sung needed was a reliable supplier who would exchange products for cash with no strings attached. Pakistan proved to be exactly that.

Since 1976 the relationship between Pakistan and North Korea has evolved into a partnership. Benazir Bhutto confirmed it. In 1993 – while she was Pakistan's prime minister – she said that A. Q. Khan had asked her to go to Pyongyang to ask the North Koreans to give Pakistan the Nodong missiles, a medium-range ballistic missile that the DPRK had developed in the mid-1980s. Pakistan had the bomb, he said, but did not have a similar missile to deliver it deep inside India. Bhutto did what she had been asked to do and got the missiles.[8]

North Korea proved to be much more than a nuclear client for Pakistan because of its military achievements. The DPRK has assembled a massive military machine and, being very good at reverse engineering, it had been manufacturing its own weapons. Because North Korea is believed to have the fourth-largest army in the world, more than one US president has ruled out any intervention in the country because of the serious consequences it would cause, both in terms of lives lost and length of the conflict.

In 1994, President Bill Clinton considered a pre-emptive strike on North Korea's Yongbyon nuclear reactor, but the Pentagon concluded it would trigger a conflict that could easily require four months of high-intensity combat and involve more than 600,000 South Korean troops and half a million US reinforcements to those already stationed in South Korea. According to Don Oberdorfer, a former *Washington Post* reporter, advisers to Bill Clinton predicted 52,000 US casualties in the first ninety days of combat alone (in the entire Vietnam War 58,000 American soldiers died).[9] Some estimates went as far as forecasting a total of a million casualties during the conflict, not to mention the economic damage and war-related costs that could run into trillions of dollars. President Obama also considered surgical strikes but, as David Sanger and William Broad reported in the *New York Times*, obtaining timely intelligence was nearly impossible and 'the risks of missing were tremendous, including renewed war on the Korean Peninsula'.[10]

Donald Trump has blamed his predecessors for not dealing with North Korea in the last quarter of a century. But he has reassured the world that he will fix the mess. The challenge is bigger than ever before: Trump faces a regime that we now know has a nuclear device and most probably is very close to carrying it as far as the USA. In September 2017 Kim Jong-un's nuclear scientists tested a hydrogen bomb that is believed to be ten times more destructive than Hiroshima. North Korea's propaganda boasted that the bomb was small enough to be fitted on a long-range missile. And the DPRK has such a missile.

On 4 July 2017, America's Independence Day, North Korea tested the Hwason 14 missile, a mobile inter-continental ballistic missile developed by the DPRK and operated exclusively by it. The missile can travel 10,000 kilometres, which means most of America is in its range (Seattle is just 5,000 kilometres away).

In retrospect, it seems that the Bush administration toppled the wrong dictator.

The Comfort of Nukes

North Korea's passion for nukes springs from the trauma of the Korean War. In 1958, in the aftermath of the conflict, the United States installed hundreds of nuclear weapons in South Korea with the clear message that it would use them at the beginning of an invasion of the North should it decide to. Americans and South Koreans have staged regular military exercises across the border of North Korea and at sea to rehearse this invasion. North Koreans have lived with the fear of another war for decades. Paradoxically, these intimidation tactics have strengthened the DPRK regime. The Kim dynasty has used the politics of fear to its own advantage, presenting itself as the sole guarantor of peace against its enemies – South Korea and the United States.

Against this scenario, building and possessing the atomic bomb became a necessity for North Korea to survive and protect itself. The popular acceptance of the phenomenal effort and sacrifices made for the nuclear program relies on this view. North Korea is not the sole country to have successfully linked a nuclear program to defence of the status quo. All states at odds with nuclear powers, for example, Pakistan versus India, have sought nuclear capability to guarantee their own survival. The idea that North Korea or Iran might strike first and attack America with nuclear weapons is highly unlikely; the purpose of building an atomic bomb is not to launch it against the United States but to prevent an attack by the USA or any other country. The reason is simple: everybody knows that a nuclear attack against the United States or its allies by countries like North Korea and Iran, or anybody else, would provoke the immediate destruction of those regimes.

Following this logic, the building of every new nuclear weapon creates a greater guarantee of the survival of the state that possesses it and furthers stability, because it will never be used. Although the *deterrence* factor of the Cold War era – both superpowers possessing the atomic bomb – would appear to belong to the past, it continues to exist between legitimate and rogue nuclear states. Since 9/11, this renewed thinking about nuclear deterrence has gained strength and convinced the North Koreans that the nuclear program is fundamental to their survival and that renouncing it is suicidal. Vladimir Putin has illustrated this concept.

> Everybody remembers what happened to Iraq and Saddam Hussein. Saddam abandoned the production of weapons of mass destruction. Nevertheless, under the pretext of searching for these weapons, Saddam Hussein himself and his family were killed. [...] The country was destroyed and Saddam Hussein was hanged. Everybody is aware of it and everybody remembers it. The North Koreans are also aware of it and remember it.[11]

The North Koreans often mention what happened to Mohammed Gadhafi. When he agreed to give up his pursuit of nuclear, chemical and biological weapons, Bush promised that if other countries would do the same, the USA would offer an open path to better relationships. However, eight years later, the USA and NATO contributed to the overthrow of Gadhafi, who was eventually killed. The North Korean leadership has described the diplomatic efforts to persuade Colonel Gadhafi to give up his arsenal of unconventional weapons as an invasion tactic.

From North Korea's perspective, what has happened in the Middle East confirms that the DPRK should never give up its nukes. And this explains why Kim Jong-un has not paid any attention to the promises of economic cooperation in exchange for the dismantling of North Korea's nuclear program. On the contrary, he has accelerated it, ramping up missile testing. Since he assumed power, at the age of twenty-seven, Kim Jong-un has tested eighty-four missiles – more than double the number that his father and grandfather tested. The North Korean leadership is also convinced that the nuclear deterrence guarantees the survival of the regime in the eventuality of an internal revolt, as happened in Libya. Indeed, foreign powers will think twice before arming the rebels if Pyongyang possesses nuclear weapons.[12]

So far deterrence has worked for the DPRK not only to keep its enemies at bay but also, paradoxically, to lure the West into helping the regime survive. In the second half of the 1990s, Kim Jong-il used the nuclear program as a bargaining chip to get food, oil and other forms of assistance from the West. He succeeded in stringing along more than one US administration by playing the deterrence game. In the ultimate analysis, deterrence is a confidence game; to be effective, you need to convince people that, if they step over the line, you really will do the things you say you'll do. Washington has to believe that Pyongyang would do to Tokyo or Seoul what it has said it would and Pyongyang has to believe Washington would use the bomb.

So far North Korea has succeeded because it is unpredictable. Its behaviour is at odds with the rest of the world and nobody feels confident ruling out a nuclear strike. Donald Trump is the fourth president of the United States who has promised to end North Korea's nuclear program. Bill Clinton signed a deal in which North Korea agreed to freeze its nuclear development in exchange for oil and a civilian reactor, but neither side fulfilled its commitments and North Korea outsmarted the USA. George W. Bush initially refused bilateral negotiations but then changed his mind and joined the Six-Party Talks.[13] Barack Obama first appeared conciliatory then retreated into a stonewalling policy called 'strategic patience'. Finally, during his first nine months at the White House, Donald Trump led the UN Security Council to pass several rounds of additional sanctions against North Korea, but it seems like this has only made Kim more determined.

Will Kim Jong-un outsmart the USA and the world as his grandfather and father did and achieve their dream, a nuclearised DPRK?

The Art of Deceit

Since its birth, the DPRK has succeeded in fooling its enemies, stringing along several US administrations and proving to have mastered 'the art of deceit'.

In 1985 the Democratic People's Republic of Korea signed the Nuclear Non-proliferation Treaty, allowing international inspectors into most of its nuclear sites. That gave Pyongyang the breathing space to secretly gain access to the technology it needed to continue to build a nuclear device. In 1993 the International Atomic Energy Agency's inspection team came to the conclusion that the DPRK had broken the treaty at least three times, in 1989, 1990 and 1991. At that point negotiations started with the Clinton administration to resolve the crisis, which led to the signature of the Agreed Framework in 1994. In exchange for freezing their nuclear program, the North Koreans would get two light-water reactors and shipments of heavy fuel oil from the Americans. The USA also agreed to work towards a normalisation of diplomatic relationships between the two countries. Building on this agreement, by 2000 the negotiations had progressed to the point that some analysts believed there was a good chance to end the conflict between the DPRK and South Korea and the USA. They were wrong: at the eleventh hour Bill Clinton did not travel to North Korea, he never shook Kim Jong-il's hand.

Neither the Americans or the North Koreans had any intention of honouring the deal. The USA never fully lifted economic sanctions against North Korea and did not attempt to normalise diplomatic relations. As John Feffer and John Gershman write,

> The Clinton administration persuaded Congress to accept the construction of two light-water reactors in North Korea by arguing, quietly, that the regime in Pyongyang would not likely be around in 2003 when the reactors were supposed to go online. Instead, the regime is still around.[14]

While Clinton was bluffing, the North Koreans were deceiving everybody by continuing to work at the nuclear program with the help of Pakistan. A June 2002 CIA report mentioned that Pakistan had been bartering nuclear weapons secrets for North Korean missile systems, including data on how to build and test a uranium-triggered nuclear weapon.[15]

Kim Jong-un is a third-generation Kim who is fully committed to the nuclear program. He may also be the one who succeeds in transforming the DPRK into a nuclear power. He hinted at this in his first speech in April 2012 when he said, 'superiority in military technology is no longer monopolised by imperialists and the time in which enemies threaten us with nuclear weapons has passed for ever'.[16] To prove this point, he needs a long-range missile capable of travelling to the USA – which he got – and a nuclear warhead small enough to fit on it – which he claims he has. If the DPRK has not achieved a proper miniaturisation of the nuclear bomb yet, it is only a matter of time until it does. It has the expertise and the capacity, something it acquired in the aftermath of the implosion of the Soviet Union, when Western countries were too busy congratulating themselves on the Cold War victory to pay attention to North Korea.

Bruce Klingner, former CIA expert on Korea, claims that when the Soviet Union imploded, the DPRK was able to employ top rocket and nuclear scientists, and possibly as many as ten of them moved to North Korea.[17] These are scientists who have been working at its nuclear program. Pyongyang also used its spies to steal missile technology from missile factories in the former Soviet bloc. A 2011 video from the Ukraine secret service, for example, shows two North Koreans copying plans inside a long-range missile factory in the Ukraine. What the North Koreans wanted was the Soviet engine for long-range missiles, which was produced both in Russia and in the Ukraine. The Hwason 14 proves that they got this technology and have built on it, developing their own advanced technical know-how for long-range missiles and, possibly, for miniaturising a nuclear device. The self-reliance motto has been applied to the nuclear program.

The DPRK has also been building a network of facilities where nuclear scientists work around the clock. These are mostly underground, hence nobody really knows how big they are. The only way to spy on buildings is from above, from satellite pictures, says Curtis Melvin of the US–Korea Institute at Johns Hopkins University.[18] According to his research, most of the secret nuclear test sites are on the east coast. A vast network of tunnels has been built underneath the mountains and this is where North Korea has conducted most of its nuclear tests. The main nuclear research facility is Pungye-Ri, about 600 kilometres north of Pyongyang, and this is where the scientists live.

When put in the context of the economic sanctions, North Korea's achievements in building a functioning nuclear program seem to prove that the sanctions have not worked. South Korea estimates that the DPRK spends between $1 billion and $3 billion per year to keep the nuclear program going. Its total cost of defence is estimated at $10 billion per year. This is a fraction of what the USA spends, however, for North Korea it is a quarter to a third of its GDP ($30–40 billion).[19] Can North Korea afford to carry on this expenditure? Curtis Melvin believes it can. 'This is expensive, but probably it is a cost the country can absorb without fomenting much resentment among the North Korean elites', he says. 'In fact, North Korean elites would probably feel less secure without a nuclear program, even if its costs relative to the economy as a whole were higher.' Melvin says the economic situation for ordinary North Koreans would have to be in near ruin, with domestic resentment among elites reaching dangerous levels, before the leadership would reconsider its nuclear program. 'Current signals indicate that North Korea is nowhere near this breaking point.'[20]

A Western diplomat who lived in North Korea disagrees with these estimates.

> I think these are wrong estimates given the fact that DPRK's external trade is anywhere in the range of 3 to 6 billion US dollars. One has to keep in mind that the main part, which is the labour force, is for free or at no more cost then food and clothing. How would 1 to 3 billion dollars be used on (imported) hardware? That's not possible, keeping in mind that also hardware from within the DPRK is considered to be no cost. The real cost is reflected in the fact that the people aren't given the prosperity they would deserve for the labour they provide to their state. I think these estimates are based on a full cost model applicable to our capitalistic system where everything can be labelled with a price tag.

In any case, completing the nuclear program will allow the leadership to reduce the total defence budget because the nuclear device will be a better deterrent and less costly than conventional weapons. Money could be allocated for infrastructure and to improve people's living standards or could be used to offset the impact of the latest round of sanctions. So the idea that Kim Jong-un may be convinced at this point to renounce the nuclear dream of his father and grandfather is a fantasy. The nuclear program remains a top priority.

Epilogue

The Future

Experts and the media are concerned about the clash of propaganda between Donald Trump and Kim Jong-un. Both are new to the game of politics and seem to have a narcissistic approach to it. Neither of them appears to be able or willing to engage in diplomacy and they both enjoy throwing insults at each other.

Regardless of personality clashes, Kim Jong-un will continue to test the red line that separates the DPRK from the rest of the world. Donald Trump has at his disposal three possible scenarios. The first one is decapitation, that is, a surgical strike to kill Kim Jong-un. David Maxwell, a former US special forces colonel who fought in the Korean War, does not believe that will work. The system is constructed to protect Kim. There are three rings of defence around him; by the time the strike takes place he will be somewhere underground. The second option is a strike against North Korea's missile nuclear facilities, but many are hidden underground and there is not sufficient intelligence to know where they are actually located. Any of these strikes would trigger retaliation from Pyongyang, including the use of a nuclear device, if not against the USA, then against South Korea or Japan. Let's not forget that North Korea has a large display of heavy artillery positioned across the border with South Korea.

The only viable option seems to be diplomacy. So far the USA has put pressure upon China to increase the sanctions, but China will never abandon North Korea, its role as a buffer across its border is too important. Even if in recent months China has appeared to be much tougher on the DPRK, in the long run it will continue to do business with Pyongyang. The only viable option seems to be diplomacy. A possible solution, and the one that will guarantee peace, is to accept the DPRK into the nuclear club. Not an option that Trump would normally consider, unless the man who has mastered the art of the deal strikes the deal of the millennium with the nation that perfected the art of deceit: North Korea.

Appendix A

War of Tweets and Nuclear Missile Tests between Trump and Kim

Trump's quotes are compiled from his tweets and published interviews.

1999

Trump: *First, I'd negotiate. I would negotiate like crazy and I'd make sure that we try to get the best deal possible...These people in three or four years they're going to be having nuclear weapons. They're going to have those weapons pointed all over the world and specifically at the United States and wouldn't you be better off solving...the biggest problem this world has is nuclear proliferation and we have a country like there, North Korea, which is sort of wacko, not a bunch of dummies and they are going out and they are developing nuclear weapons...and wouldn't it be good to go out and really negotiate something?*

2013

North Korea's National Defense Commission admits that it will continue nuclear testing and long-range rocket launches. The tests and launches will feed into an 'upcoming all-out action' targeting the United States, 'the sworn enemy of the Korean people', the commission says.

Trump: *'Think of yourself as a one-man army. You're not only the commander in chief, you're the soldier as well.'* – *Think Like a Billionaire.*

North Korea conducts its third nuclear test. This is the first nuclear test carried out under Kim Jong-un.

Trump: *Negotiation is persuasion more than power. Be reasonable and flexible, and never let anyone know exactly where you're coming from.*

Angered by the UN Security Council sanctions over its nuclear test, North Korea threatens for the first time to launch a pre-emptive nuclear strike against the USA and South Korea.

Trump: *How much is South Korea paying the US for protection against North Korea???? NOTHING!*

Pyongyang cuts its last military hotline with South Korea.

Trump: *What do we get from our economic competitor South Korea for the tremendous cost of protecting them from North Korea? – NOTHING!*

Pyongyang says it will soon have rockets aimed at US targets and releases photos that show Kim Jong-un meeting with military officials discussing nuclear strike plans on a US map.

Trump: *North Korea can't survive, or even eat, without the help of China. China could solve this problem with one phone call – they love taunting us!*

North Korea declares that it will restart the Yongbyon nuclear complex, including a uranium enrichment plant and a reactor that was shut down under the October 2007 agreement with the United States and four other nations. US Secretary of State John Kerry warns that the United States will not accept that North Korea will become a 'nuclear state'.

Trump: *Where is the President? [Obama] It is time for him to come on TV and show strength against the repeated threats from North Korea – and others.*

2014

North Korea warns that it is preparing another nuclear test and fires hundreds of shells across the maritime DMZ line. In response, South Korea fires about 300 shells into North Korean waters and sends fighter jets to the border.

Trump: *Our President must be very careful with the 28 year old wack job in North Korea. At some point we may have to get very tough-blatant threats.*

2015

In an exclusive interview with CNN, the deputy director of a North Korean think tank says the country has the missile capability to strike mainland United States and would do so if the United States 'forced their hand'.

Trump: *Dennis Rodman was either drunk or on drugs (delusional) when he said I wanted to go to North Korea with him. Glad I fired him on Apprentice!*

North Korea says that it has the ability to miniaturise nuclear weapons, a key step towards building nuclear missiles. A US National Security Council spokesperson responds that the United States does not think the North Koreans have that capability.

Trump: *Nobody ever mentions North Korea where you have this maniac sitting there and he actually has nuclear weapons and somebody better start thinking about North Korea and perhaps a couple of other places. But certainly North Korea.*

Yes. Yes. [on whether he bites back 'pretty hard'] I wouldn't be nuking anybody. I will have a military that's so strong and powerful, and so respected, we're not gonna have to nuke anybody. We wouldn't get rid of the weapons. Because you have so many people out there. But I would be somebody that would be amazingly calm under pressure. I just don't want to talk about it. It is highly, highly, highly, highly unlikely that I would ever be using them.

North Korea state media announces that the country has added the hydrogen bomb to its arsenal.

Trump: *I think we need somebody, absolutely, that we can trust, who is totally responsible, who really knows what he or she is doing. That is so powerful and so important. But we have to be extremely vigilant and extremely careful when it comes to nuclear. Nuclear changes the whole ball game. For me, nuclear, the power, the devastation, is very important to me.*

The biggest problem this world has today is not President Obama with global warming, which is inconceivable, this is what he's saying. The biggest problem we have is nuclear – nuclear proliferation and having some maniac, having some madman go out and get a nuclear weapon. That's in my opinion, that is the single biggest problem that our country faces right now.

2016

North Korea announces that it has successfully tested the hydrogen bomb. A day after the alleged test, White House spokesperson Josh Earnest says that the United States had not been able to verify that the test was indeed successful.

Trump: *I would get China to make that guy [Kim Jong-un] disappear in one form or another very quickly.*

China is sucking us dry. They're taking our money, they're taking our jobs and doing so much. We have rebuilt China with what they've taken out. We have power over China. China should do that.

Well, you know, I've heard of worse things, frankly. I mean this guy's a bad dude – and don't underestimate him. Any young guy that can take over from his father with all those generals and everybody else that probably wants the position, this is not somebody to be underestimated.

North Korea announces that it has miniaturised nuclear warheads that can fit on ballistic missiles.

Trump: *Right now we're protecting, we're basically protecting Japan, and we are, every time North Korea raises its head, you know, we get calls from Japan and we get calls from everybody else, and 'Do something.' And there'll be a point at which we're just not going to be able to do it anymore. Now, does that mean nuclear? It could mean nuclear. It's a very scary nuclear world. Biggest problem, to me, in the world, is nuclear, and proliferation.*

Trump: *At some point, we cannot be the policeman of the world. And unfortunately, we have a nuclear world now. And you have, Pakistan has them. You have, probably, North Korea has them. I mean, they don't have delivery yet, but you know, probably, I mean to me, that's a big problem. And, would I rather have North Korea have them with Japan sitting there having them also? You may very well be better off if that's the case.*

North Korea claims to have detonated a nuclear warhead. According to South Korea's Meteorological Administration, the blast is estimated to have the explosive power of 10 kilotons.

Trump: *Clinton is weak on North Korea.*

The United States must greatly strengthen and expand its nuclear capability until such time as the world comes to its senses regarding nukes.

2017

North Korea successfully tested a land-based KN-15 missile, a new solid-fuel intermediate-range missile, which travelled 310 miles into the Sea of Japan.

Trump: *It would be wonderful, a dream would be that no country would have nukes, but if countries are going to have nukes, we're going to be at the top of the pack.*

A KN-17 missile launch occurred while Japanese Prime Minister Shinzo Abe met with Trump at Mar-a-Lago, during which the pair discussed how to curb North Korea's missile and nuclear programs.

Trump: *I am the first one that would like to see everybody – nobody have nukes, but we're never going to fall behind any country even if it's a friendly country, we're never going to fall behind on nuclear power.*

North Korea fired a KN-17 for the third time in April. The missile travelled 21 miles before breaking up in mid-air, according to a US official.

Trump: *People are saying: 'Is he sane?' I have no idea...but he was a young man of 26 or 27...when his father died. He's dealing with obviously very tough people, in particular the generals and others.*

And at a very young age, he was able to assume power. A lot of people, I'm sure, tried to take that power away, whether it was his uncle or anybody else. And he was able to do it. So obviously, he's a pretty smart cookie.

North Korea launched, for the first time, a two-stage intercontinental ballistic missile to mark 4 July.

Trump: *North Korea has just launched another missile. Does this guy have anything better to do with his life? Hard to believe that South Korea and Japan will put up with this much longer. Perhaps China will put a heavy move on North Korea and end this nonsense once and for all!*

Trade between China and North Korea grew almost 40% in the first quarter. So much for China working with us — but we had to give it a try!

After many years of failure, countries are coming together to finally address the dangers posed by North Korea. We must be tough and decisive!

Military solutions are now fully in place, locked and loaded, should North Korea act unwisely. Hopefully Kim Jong Un will find another path!

North Korea fires a ballistic missile over Japan that prompts the government in Tokyo to warn residents in its path to take cover.

Trump: *My first order as President was to renovate and modernize our nuclear arsenal. It is now far stronger and more powerful than ever before...Hopefully we will never have to use this power, but there will never be a time that we are not the most powerful nation in the world!*

The country's state-run Korean Central News Agency reports that Kim Jong-un has presided over the launch of an 'ultra-modern rocket system', the first missile ever fired from the capital, Pyongyang.

North Korean officials tell CNN in Pyongyang that Kim Jong-un is 'very satisfied with the performance of the missile'.

The North Korean launch is 'the first step of the military operation of the [North Korean military] in the Pacific and a meaningful prelude to containing Guam', state media says.

Trump: *The US has been talking to North Korea, and paying them extortion money, for 25 years. Talking is not the answer!*

The United States is considering, in addition to other options, stopping all trade with any country doing business with North Korea.

South Korea is finding, as I have told them, that their talk of appeasement with North Korea will not work, they only understand one thing!

North Korea has conducted a major Nuclear Test. Their words and actions continue to be very hostile and dangerous to the United States.

North Korea is a rogue nation which has become a great threat and embarrassment to China, which is trying to help but with little success.

North Korea says it successfully conducted a test of a hydrogen bomb, the country's sixth nuclear test. The explosion created a magnitude-6.3 tremor, making it the most powerful weapon Pyongyang has ever tested.

Trump: *I spoke with President Moon of South Korea last night. Asked how Rocket Man is doing. Long gas lines forming in North Korea. Too bad!*

After allowing North Korea to research and build Nukes while Secretary of State (Bill C also), Crooked Hillary now criticizes.

Today, I announced a new Executive Order with re: to North Korea. We must all do our part to ensure the complete denuclearization of #NoKo.

Kim Jong Un of North Korea, who is obviously a madman, who doesn't mind starving or killing his people, will be tested like never before!

Just heard Foreign Minister of North Korea speak at UN. If he echoes thoughts of Little Rocket Man, they won't be around much longer!

Iran just test-fired a Ballistic Missile capable of reaching Israel. They are also working with North Korea. Not much of an agreement we have!

22 September

Kim Jong-un, as chairman of the State Affairs Commission of the DPRK, releases a statement:

> The mentally deranged behaviour of the US president openly expressing on the UN arena the unethical will to 'totally destroy' a sovereign state, beyond the boundary of threats of regime change or overturn of social system, makes even those with normal thinking faculty think about discretion and composure.

Now that Trump has denied the existence of and insulted me and my country in front of the eyes of the world and made the most ferocious declaration of a war in history, that he would destroy the DPRK, we will consider with seriousness exercising a corresponding, highest level of hard-line countermeasure in history.

Action is the best option in treating the dotard who, hard of hearing, is uttering only what he wants to say. I will surely and definitely tame the mentally deranged US dotard with fire.

7 October

Trump: *Presidents and their administrations have been talking to North Korea for 25 years, agreements made and massive amounts of money paid hasn't worked, agreements violated before the ink was dry, making fools of U.S. negotiators. Sorry, but only one thing will work!*

9 October

Trump: *Our country has been unsuccessfully dealing with North Korea for 25 years, giving billions of dollars and getting nothing. Policy didn't work!*

13 October

North Korea renews a threat to launch missiles towards the US territory of Guam, warning that 'reckless moves' by the USA would compel Pyongyang to take action. 'We have already warned several times that we will take counteractions for self-defense, including a salvo of missiles into waters near the US territory of Guam', states Kim Kwang Hak, a researcher at the Institute for American Studies of the North Korean Foreign Ministry, as reported by the Korean Central News Agency (KCNA). 'The US military action hardens our determination that the US should be tamed with fire and lets us take our hand closer to the "trigger" for taking the toughest countermeasure.'

15 October

In a KCNA report, North Korea says Trump is trying to bring the world to the 'brink of war': 'The US is the war merchant and strangler of peace which gives rise to dispute and conflicts around the world in order to draw water to its mill regardless of the existence of mankind.'

7 November

Trump (to the National Assembly of the Republic of Korea):

> North Korea is a country ruled as a cult. At the centre of this military cult is a deranged belief in the leader's destiny to rule as parent protector over a conquered Korean peninsula and an enslaved Korean people.
>
> The regime has interpreted America's past restraint as weakness. This would be a fatal miscalculation. This is a very different administration than the United States has had in the past.
>
> Today, I hope I speak not only for our countries, but for all civilised nations, when I say to the North: Do not underestimate us, and do not try us. We will defend our common security, our shared prosperity and our sacred liberty.

America does not seek conflict or confrontation, but we will never run from it. History is filled with discarded regimes that have foolishly tested America's resolve. Anyone who doubts the strength or determination of the United States should look to our past, and you will doubt it no longer. We will not permit America or our allies to be blackmailed or attacked. We will not allow American cities to be threatened with destruction. We will not be intimidated. And we will not let the worst atrocities in history be repeated here, on this ground, we fought and died so hard to secure.

The time for excuses is over. Now is the time for strength. If you want peace, you must stand strong at all times.

It is our responsibility and our duty to confront this danger together – because the longer we wait, the greater the danger grows, and the fewer the options become.

North Korea is not the paradise your grandfather envisioned. It is a hell that no person deserves. Yet, despite every crime you have committed against God and man, we are ready to offer, and we will do that – we will offer a path to a much better future. It begins with an end to the aggression of your regime, a stop to your development of ballistic missiles, and complete, verifiable and total denuclearisation.

9 November

Trump: *My meetings with President Xi Jinping were very productive on both trade and the subject of North Korea. He is a highly respected and powerful representative of his people. It was great being with him and Madame Peng Liyuan!*

11 November

Trump: *Why would Kim Jong-un insult me by calling me "old,"* *when I would NEVER call him "short and fat?" Oh well, I try* *so hard to be his friend — and maybe someday that will happen!*

15 November

North Korea's state media criticises Trump for insulting leader Kim Jong-un, saying the US president deserves the death penalty and calling him a coward for cancelling a visit to the inter-Korean border.

An editorial in the ruling party newspaper *Rodong Sinmun* focuses its anger on Trump's visit to South Korea the previous week, during which he denounced the North's 'cruel dictatorship' in a speech to legislators in Seoul.

'The worst crime for which he can never be pardoned is that he dared [to] malignantly hurt the dignity of the supreme leadership', the editorial says. 'He should know that he is just a hideous criminal sentenced to death by the Korean people.'

20 November

Trump designates North Korea a 'state sponsor of terrorism' in a meeting with his Cabinet at the White House.

Appendix B

North Korea Timeline

1945   After World War II, the Japanese occupation of Korea ends with the partition of the Korean peninsula at the 38th parallel. Soviet troops occupy the north and US troops occupy the south.

1946   North Korea's communist party, called the Korean Workers' Party, is born. With Soviet backing, Kim Il-sung becomes the leader of the new party.

1948   Kim Il-sung declares the birth of the Democratic People's Republic of Korea. Soviet troops withdraw from North Korea. At the same time, the Republic of Korea is established in South Korea, but neither government recognises the other.

1950   Seventy-five thousand soldiers from the North invade the South, triggering the Korean War. The conflict lasts for three years with the USA backing the South, and China and the USSR backing the North.

1953   North and South Korea sign an armistice. The Korean Demilitarised Zone is established very close to the 38th parallel.

1972   North and South Korea issue joint statements on peaceful reunification. The first formal meeting between the North and the South is held. Kim Il-sung says that peaceful reunification is desired as 'early as possible'.

1974   Kim Il-sung designates his eldest son, Kim Jong-il, as his successor. A North Korean agent attempts to assassinate South Korean President, Park Chung-hee, who survives, but his wife is killed.

1977   Nationalisation of land property.

1985   North Korea joins the international Nuclear Non-proliferation Treaty, barring the country from producing nuclear weapons.

1986   The research nuclear reactor in Yongbyon becomes operational.

China and North Korea establish protocol on security in the border area.

1987   North Korea is accused of blowing up the South Korean civilian airliner, Korean Air Flight 858, 115 people are killed.

1991   North and South Korea join the United Nations.

1993   The International Atomic Energy Agency accuses North Korea of violating the Nuclear Non-proliferation Treaty and demands inspectors to be given access to nuclear waste storage sites. North Korea threatens to quit the treaty.

North Korea test fires a medium-range Rodong ballistic missile into the Sea of Japan.

1994   Kim il-Sung suffers a heart attack and dies in July. Kim Jong-il succeeds his father as leader, but does not take over the role of president yet.

North Korea and the USA sign an Agreed Framework under which Pyongyang commits to freezing its nuclear program in return for heavy fuel oil and two light-water nuclear reactors.

1996   North Korea announces it will no longer abide by the armistice that ended the Korean War, and sends thousands of troops into the Demilitarised Zone.

A North Korean submarine with 26 commandos and crew on board runs aground near the South Korean town of Gangneung. All but one onboard is killed along with 17 South Koreans following several skirmishes.

1998   Former President Kim-il Sung is declared eternal president. Kim Jong-il expands his powers and becomes head of state. The UN delivers aid.

South Korea captures a North Korean submarine in its waters. The crew is found dead inside.

North Korea fires a multistage long-range rocket that flies over Japan and lands in the Pacific Ocean, the rocket is well beyond North Korea's known capability.

2000   Landmark inter-Korean summit takes place in Pyongyang between Kim Jong-il and South Korean President Kim Dae-jung, paving the way for the reopening of border liaison offices and family reunions. The South also grants amnesty to over 3,500 North Korean prisoners.

2002 US President George W. Bush labels North Korea, Iraq and Iran an 'axis of evil' for continuing to build 'weapons of mass destruction'.

North and South Korean naval vessels wage a gun battle in the Yellow Sea. Some 30 North Korean and four South Korean sailors are killed.

Japanese Prime Minister Junichiro Koizumi makes an historic visit to North Korea, during which the regime admits to having abducted 13 Japanese citizens in the 1970s and 1980s and that at least four are still alive.

The USA and its key Asian allies Japan and South Korea stop oil shipments following North Korea's reported admission that it has secretly been developing a uranium-based nuclear program.

North Korea announces it is reactivating nuclear facilities at Yongbyon and expels UN inspectors.

2003 North Korea withdraws from the Nuclear Non-proliferation Treaty, marking the start of a series of Six-Party Talks involving China, the Koreas, the USA, Japan and Russia to try to resolve the nuclear issue.

North Korea withdraws from the 1992 agreement with South Korea to keep the Korean peninsula free of nuclear weapons.

Pyongyang declares it has completed the reprocessing of 8,000 spent nuclear fuel rods. Experts say this would give the North enough weapons-grade plutonium to develop up to six nuclear bombs within months.

2005　Pyongyang admits that it has produced nuclear warheads for 'self-defence'.

2006　North Korea test fires seven missiles including a long-range Taepodong-2 missile, which crashes shortly after take-off despite it reportedly having the capability to hit the USA.

North Korea conducts its first nuclear weapons test at an underground facility. The blast has an explosive force of less than 1 kilotonne, leading many to think that it 'fizzled' rather than detonated properly.

The UN imposes economic and commercial sanctions on North Korea.

2007　Second inter-Korean summit held in Pyongyang. President Roh Moo-hyun becomes the first South Korean leader to walk across the DMZ separating North and South in the first meeting in 15 years.

Passenger trains cross the North–South Korean border for first time in 56 years.

2008　North–South relations deteriorate sharply after new South Korean President Lee Myung-bak promises to take a harder line on North Korea.

Kim Jong-il suffers a stroke.

North Korea agrees to provide full access to Yongbyon nuclear site after the USA removes it from terrorism blacklist.

2009   North Korea says it is scrapping all military and political deals with the South, accusing it of 'hostile intent'.

North Korea launches a long-range rocket, carrying what it says is a communications satellite; its neighbours accuse it of testing long-range missile technology. Condemnation from the UN Security Council prompts North Korea to walk out of Six-Party Talks and restart its nuclear facilities.

North Korea carries out its second underground nuclear test. The UN Security Council condemns move in June.

North Korea frees American journalists Laura Ling and Euna Lee after former US President Bill Clinton facilitates their release. The pair was sentenced to 12 years' hard labour for allegedly crossing the border illegally.

North Korea makes conciliatory gestures to South Korea, sending a delegation to the funeral of former President Kim Dae-jung, releasing four South Korean fishermen and agreeing to resume family reunions.

North Korea's state-run news agency reports the reprocessing of 8,000 spent fuel rods is complete, garnering enough weapons-grade plutonium for one to two nuclear bombs.

2010   Increased social unrest reportedly leads the government to relax free market restrictions after a 2009 currency revaluation wiped out many cash savings in the country.

North Korea sinks South Korean warship *Cheonan* near sea border.

Kim Jong-il's youngest son, Kim Jong-un, is appointed to senior political and military posts, fuelling speculation of a possible succession.

North Korea reportedly shows an eminent visiting American nuclear scientist a new, secretly built facility for enriching uranium at its Yongbyon complex. The revelation sparks alarm and anger in the USA, South Korea and Japan.

A cross-border clash near disputed maritime border results in the deaths of two South Korean marines. North Korea's military insists it did not open fire first and blames the South for the incident.

2011   Kim Jong-il dies. Kim Jong-un presides at the funeral of his father and takes over.

2012   A rocket launch – viewed internationally as a banned test of long-range Taepodong-2 missile technology – fails. North Korea says the aim was to put a satellite into orbit to mark the 100th birth anniversary of Kim Il-sung.

Ri Yong-ho is removed as the army head; Kim Jong-un appoints himself the commander in chief.

North Korea claims it has missiles that can hit the US mainland after South Korea and Washington announce a deal to extend the range of South Korea's ballistic missiles.

North Korea successfully launches a 'rocket-mounted satellite' into orbit following a failed attempt in April.

2013 The UN approves fresh sanctions after North Korea stages its third nuclear test, said to be more powerful than the 2009 test.

North Korea says it will restart all facilities at its main Yongbyon nuclear complex and briefly withdraws its 53,000-strong workforce from the South Korean-funded Kaesong joint industrial park, stalling operations at 123 South Korean factories.

Panama impounds a North Korean ship carrying two MiG-21 jet fighters under bags of sugar. The UN later blacklists the ship's operator.

China bans export to North Korea of items that could be used to make missiles or nuclear, chemical and biological weapons.

Kim Jong-un's uncle, Chang Song-thaek, is found guilty of attempting to overthrow the state and is summarily executed in a purge seen as the biggest shake-up since the death of Kim Jong-il.

2014 North Korea test fires two medium-range Rodong ballistic missiles for the first time since 2009, in violation of UN resolutions and just hours after the USA, South Korea and Japan meet in the Netherlands for talks.

North Korean officials pay a surprise visit to South Korea and agree to resume formal talks that have been suspended since February.

North Korea and the USA exchange accusations of cyberattacks over a Sony Pictures film mocking Kim Jong-un, prompting new US sanctions the following month.

2015   South Korea halts loudspeaker propaganda broadcasts across the Demilitarised Zone after the North fires on them during the annual US–South Korean military exercises.

North Korea confirms it has put its Yongbyon nuclear plant – mothballed in 2007 – back into operation.

The USA imposes new sanctions on North Korea over weapons proliferation, targeting the army's Strategic Rocket Force, banks and shipping companies.

2016   North Korea's announcement of the first hydrogen bomb test is met with widespread scepticism by experts.

The ruling Workers' Party holds its first congress in almost 40 years, during which Kim Jong-un is elected leader of the party.

The UN Security Council further tightens sanctions by aiming to cut one of North Korea's main exports, coal, by 60%.

2017   Kim Jong-un says North Korea is in the final stages of developing long-range guided missiles capable of carrying nuclear warheads.

Kim Jong-un's estranged half-brother, Kim Jong-nam, is killed by a highly toxic nerve agent in Malaysia, with investigators suspecting North Korean involvement.

Pyongyang test fires a long-range missile into the Sea of Japan, with some experts admitting that the missile could potentially reach Alaska. A US aircraft carrier is moved into the area, escalating tensions between Washington and Pyongyang. North Korea promises that it will retaliate 'by powerful force of arms'.

Tension rises in a war of words with the USA over a North Korean threat to fire ballistic missiles near the US Pacific territory of Guam.

China announces its plans to implement the agreed UN sanctions against North Korea, banning imports of coal, minerals and seafood.

Appendix C

South Korea Timeline

Timeline compiled from BBC and World Atlas.[1]

1945 After World War II, Japanese occupation ends with Soviet troops occupying the area north of the 38th parallel, and US troops in the south.

1948 The Republic of Korea is proclaimed.

1950–53 Korean War. South Korea is sustained by crucial US military, economic and political support. The Korean Armistice Agreement ends the Korean War; two million lives are lost.

1960 President Syngman Rhee steps down after student protests against electoral fraud. The new constitution forms the Second Republic, but political freedom remains limited. The First Republic of South Korea is overthrown in the April Revolution. Syngman Rhee is exiled.

1961 A military coup puts General Park Chung-hee in power.

1963   Park restores some political freedom and proclaims the Third Republic. A major program of industrial development begins.

1972   After secret North–South talks, both sides seek to develop dialogue aimed at unification. Park declares emergency martial law and changes the constitution allowing him to become permanent ruler.

1974   First Lady Yuk Young-soo is assassinated by North Korean Mun Segwang.

1979   US President Jimmy Carter visits South Korea and threatens to reduce US forces in Korea if Park does not stop its nuclear weapons development program. Park is assassinated. General Chun Doo-hwan seizes power the following year.

1980   Martial law declared after student demonstrations. In the city of Gwangju, the army kills at least 200 people. The Fifth Republic is formed and a new constitution is introduced.

1981   Chun is indirectly elected to a seven-year term. Martial law ends, but the government continues to have strong powers to prevent dissent. An economic shift towards computer and high-tech industries begins

1986   The constitution is changed to allow direct election of the president.

1987   Chun is pushed out of office by student unrest and international pressure in the build-up to the Sixth Constitution. General Roh Tae-woo succeeds Chun, grants a greater degree of political liberalisation and launches an anti-corruption drive.

1988   Olympic games are held in Seoul. The first free parliamentary elections are held.

1991   North and South Korea join the United Nations.

1992   People's Republic of China establish diplomatic relations.

1993   Roh is succeeded by Kim Young Sam, a former opponent of the regime and the first freely elected civilian president.

1995   Former presidents Roh Tae-woo and Chun Doo-hwan are charged with corruption and treason.

1996   South Korea is admitted to the Organisation for Economic Co-operation and Development.

1997   Asian financial crisis. South Korea reaches an agreement with the International Monetary Fund for a $55 billion bailout for the faltering economy.

1998   Kim Dae-jung is sworn in as president and pursues a 'Sunshine policy' of offering unconditional economic and humanitarian aid to North Korea.

2000   A summit is held in Pyongyang between Kim Jong-il and Kim Dae-jung. North Korea stops propaganda broadcasts against South Korea. The first visits are held between family members from North and South Korea – some had not seen each other in 50 years.

2002   The battle between South Korean and North Korean naval vessels along their disputed sea border leaves four South Koreans dead and 19 wounded. Thirty North Koreans are thought to have been killed. Roh Moo-hyun, from the governing Millennium Democratic Party, wins the closely fought presidential elections.

2003　　The biggest mass crossing of the Demilitarised Zone since the Korean War: hundreds of South Koreans travel to Pyongyang for the opening of a gymnasium funded by the South's Hyundai conglomerate. One hundred South Korean tourists fly to Pyongyang on the first flight between the two countries in more than six decades.

2004　　The USA proposes to cut its troop presence by a third. Opposition raises security fears over the plan. Parliament votes to impeach Roh Moo-hyun over a breach of election rules and incompetence, but the Constitutional Court overturns the impeachment and Roh is reinstated.

2006　　Foreign Minister Ban Ki-moon is appointed as the UN's new secretary-general. He takes office in January 2007.

2007　　South and North Korea agree to restart high-level talks suspended since July 2006 in the wake of the DPRK nuclear test. Conservative Lee Myung-bak, former Hyundai CEO, wins a landslide victory in the presidential election.

2008　　Global recession. The government announces a $130 billion financial rescue package to shore up the banking system and stabilise markets amid the global financial crisis.

President Lee Myung-bak ends the Sunshine policy; North Korea warned of catastrophic consequences. North Korea announces plans to curtail ties with South Korea, including ending the cross-border train service, based on Seoul's 'confrontational' policies.

2009   North Korea says it is scrapping all military and political deals with the South. Former South Korean president Kim Dae-jung dies; North Korea sends a senior delegation to Seoul to pay its respects.

South and North Korean warships exchange fire across a disputed sea border, and again in January 2010.

2010   North Korea accepts an offer of food aid from South Korea, the first such aid in two years.

South Korea breaks off all trade with the North shortly after the naval ship *Cheonan* is sunk by a North Korean torpedo in March. Pyongyang describes the findings as a 'fabrication' and cuts all diplomatic ties with Seoul.

2012   South Korea strikes a deal with the USA to almost triple the range of its ballistic missile system to 800 km as a response to North Korea's test of a long-range rocket in April.

South Korea elects its first female president, Park Geun-hye, of the conservative Saenuri party. She takes office in February.

2013   South Korea launches a satellite into orbit for the first time using a rocket launched from its own soil just weeks after a North Korean rocket placed a satellite in orbit.

South Korea accuses North Korea of a cyberattack that temporarily shuts down the computer systems at banks and broadcasters.

Officials from North Korea and South Korea agree to hold talks for first time since 2007.

2014 North and South Korea exchange fire into the sea across the disputed western maritime border during the largest South Korea–US military training exercise in the region for 20 years.

2015 Mass protests are held in Seoul against the government's economic policy and insistence on schools using state-approved history books.

2016 Impeachment of Park Geun-hye, who is embroiled in a political crisis over revelations that she allowed a personal friend, with no government position, to meddle in affairs of state.

2016 South Korea's military says its cyber command came under attack by North Korean hackers.

2017 The centre-left candidate Moon Jae-in is elected president in a landslide, and pledges to solve the North Korean crisis by diplomatic means.

Appendix D

North Korea Nuclear Timeline

1985
North Korea signs the Nuclear Non-proliferation Treaty (NPT).

1986
North Korea starts operation of a 5-megawatt nuclear reactor at Yongbyon after seven years of construction with Soviet help.

1993
The International Atomic Energy Agency demands that inspectors be given access to two nuclear waste storage sites. In response, North Korea threatens to quit the NPT but eventually opts to continue participating in the treaty.

1994

North Korea and the USA sign an agreement. Among other stipulations, North Korea pledges to freeze and eventually dismantle its old, graphite-moderated, plutonium-based Yongbyon nuclear reactor in exchange for international aid to build two new light-water nuclear reactors for producing electricity.

2002

US President George W. Bush labels North Korea, Iran and Iraq an 'axis of evil' in his State of the Union address. 'By seeking weapons of mass destruction, these regimes pose a grave and growing danger', he says. The Bush Administration reveals that North Korea has admitted operating a secret nuclear weapons program in violation of the 1994 agreement. The US-led consortium says it is suspending construction of the two new reactors.

2003

January North Korea withdraws from the NPT.

February The USA confirms North Korea has reactivated a 5-megawatt nuclear reactor at its Yongbyon facility, capable of producing plutonium for weapons.

April North Korea declares it has nuclear weapons.

August North Korea joins the first round of six-nation nuclear talks in Beijing, which include China, Japan, Russia, South Korea and the USA.

2005
North Korea tentatively agrees to give up its entire nuclear program, including weapons. In exchange, the USA, China, Japan, Russia and South Korea say they will provide energy assistance to North Korea as well as promote economic cooperation.

2006
July After North Korea test fires long-range missiles, the UN Security Council passes a resolution demanding that North Korea suspend the program.

October North Korea claims to have successfully tested its first nuclear weapon. The test prompts the UN Security Council to impose a broad array of sanctions.

2007
13 February North Korea agrees to close its main nuclear reactor in exchange for an aid package worth $400 million.

30 September At Six-Party Talks in Beijing, North Korea signs an agreement stating it will begin disabling its nuclear weapons facilities.

31 December North Korea misses the end-of-year deadline to disable its weapons facilities.

2008

27 June North Korea destroys a water cooling tower at the Yongbyon nuclear facility.

11 October North Korea is removed from the US list of states that sponsor terrorism.

December Six-Party Talks are held in Beijing. The talks break down over North Korea's refusal to allow international inspectors unfettered access to suspected nuclear sites.

2009

25 May North Korea announces it has conducted its second nuclear test.

12 June The UN Security Council condemns the nuclear test and imposes new sanctions.

2010

20 November A Stanford University professor publishes a report stating that North Korea has a new nuclear enrichment facility.

2011

18 February Satellite images show the North has completed a launch tower at its new west coast missile base at Tongchang-ri.

24–25 October US officials meet with a North Korean delegation in Geneva, Switzerland, in an effort to restart the six-party nuclear arms talks that broke down in 2008.

2012

29 February The US State Department announces that North Korea has agreed to a moratorium on long-range missile launches and nuclear activity at the nation's major nuclear facility in exchange for food aid.

13 April Rocket launched from Tongchang-ri appears to disintegrate soon after blastoff and falls into the ocean, South Korean authorities say.

24 May A spokesperson for South Korea's Defense Ministry says that, based on analysis of commercial satellite images at North Korea's nuclear test site, North Korea appears ready to carry out a nuclear test at any time.

12 December North Korea launches a long-range rocket, which the international community condemns as a disguised ballistic missile test.

2013

24 January North Korea's National Defense Commission says it will continue nuclear testing and long-range rocket launches in defiance of the USA. The tests and launches will feed into an 'upcoming all-out action' targeting the USA, 'the sworn enemy of the Korean people', the commission says.

12 February North Korea conducts a third nuclear test. This is the first nuclear test carried out under Kim Jong-un. Three weeks later, the UN orders additional sanctions in protest.

2014

30–31 March North Korea warns that it is prepping another nuclear test. The following day, the hostility escalates when the country fires hundreds of shells across the sea border with South Korea. In response, South Korea fires about 300 shells into North Korean waters and sends fighter jets to the border.

2015

May North Korea says it successfully test fired a submarine-launched ballistic missile, but experts say the exercise fell far short of a full flight test.

6 May In an exclusive interview with CNN, the deputy director of a North Korean think tank says the country has the missile capability to strike mainland USA and would do so if the USA 'forced their hand'.

20 May North Korea says it has the ability to miniaturise nuclear weapons, a key step towards building nuclear missiles. A US National Security Council spokesperson responds that the USA does not think North Korea has that capability.

3 December A US think tank reports that satellite images indicate North Korea is excavating a new tunnel at its main nuclear test site at Punggye-ri.

12 December North Korea state media says the country has added the hydrogen bomb to its arsenal, but Washington says it doubts Pyongyang has a thermonuclear device.

2016

6–7 January North Korea says it has successfully conducted a hydrogen bomb test. A day after the alleged test, the White House says the USA has not verified that the test was successful.

9 March North Korea announces that it has miniature nuclear warheads that can fit on ballistic missiles.

9 September North Korea claims to have detonated a nuclear warhead, its fifth suspected nuclear test, in the northeast of the country. According to South Korea's Meteorological Administration, the blast is estimated to have the explosive power of 10 kilotons.

2017

1 January In a televised address, Kim claims that North Korea could soon test an intercontinental ballistic missile that can reach the USA.

8 January US Defense Secretary Ash Carter says the military will shoot down any North Korean missile fired at the USA or any of its allies.

12 January A US defense official tells CNN that the military has deployed sea-based radar equipment to track long-range missile launches by North Korea.

15 May North Korea says a missile it has tested can carry a nuclear warhead.

29 May North Korea fires missile into Japanese waters.

4 July North Korea claims it has conducted its first successful test of an intercontinental ballistic missile that can 'reach anywhere in the world'.

25 July North Korea threatens a nuclear strike on 'the heart of the US' if it attempts to remove Kim as Supreme Leader, according to Pyongyang's state-run Korean Central News Agency (KCNA).

7 August North Korea accuses the USA of 'trying to drive the situation of the Korean peninsula to the brink of nuclear war' after the UN Security Council unanimously adopts new sanctions in response to Pyongyang's long-range ballistic missile tests last month. North Korea vows 'thousands-fold' revenge on the USA over sanctions.

9 August North Korea's military is 'examining the operational plan' to strike areas around the US territory of Guam with medium to long-range strategic ballistic missiles, KCNA says. The North Korea comments are published one day after President Donald Trump warns Pyongyang that if it continues to threaten the USA, it would face 'fire and fury like the world has never seen'.

29 August Missile fired by North Korea soars over Japan.

3 September North Korea carries out its sixth test of a nuclear weapon, causing a 6.3-magnitude seismic event, as measured by the US Geological Survey. Pyongyang claims the device is a hydrogen bomb that could be mounted on an intercontinental missile. A nuclear weapons monitoring group describes the weapon as up to eight times stronger than the bomb dropped in Hiroshima in 1945. In response to the test, Trump tweets that North Korea continues to be 'very hostile and dangerous to the United States'. He goes on to criticise South Korea, claiming that the country is engaging in 'talk of appeasement' with the North. He also says North Korea is 'an embarrassment to China', claiming Beijing is having little success reining in the Kim regime.

Notes

Prologue – Missile Crisis by Candlelight

1   Julian Borger, 'Missile crisis by candlelight: Donald Trump's use of Mar-a-Lago raises security questions', *The Guardian*, 14 February 2017, viewed 12 November 2017, <https://www.theguardian.com/us-news/2017/feb/13/mar-a-lago-north-korea-missile-crisis-trump-national-security>.

2   ibid.

3   Bruce Cumings, 'This is what's really behind North Korea's nuclear provocations', *The Nation*, 23 March 2017, viewed 12 November 2017, <https://www.thenation.com/article/this-is-whats-really-behind-north-koreas-nuclear-provocations/>.

4   Choe Sang-Hun, 'US antimissile system goes live in South Korea', *The New York Times*, 2 May 2017, viewed 12 November 2017, <https://www.nytimes.com/2017/05/02/world/asia/thaad-north-korea-missile-defense-us.html>. 'South Korea elected Moon Jae-in, a human rights lawyer who favors dialogue with North Korea, as president on Tuesday, returning the nation's liberals to power after nearly a decade in the political wilderness and setting up a potential rift with the United States over the North's nuclear weapons program.'

Chapter 1 – Going Hungry

1   David Rees, 'Introduction', in Rees, *Korea: An Illustrated History from Ancient Times to 1945*, Hippocrene Books, New York, NY, 2001.

2   The British Museum, *Reginald Campbell Thompson (Biographical Details)*, viewed 12 November 2017, <http://www.britishmuseum.

org/research/search_the_collection_database/term_details.
aspx?bioId=93633>.

3   Rees, 'The time of isolation', *Korea,* pp. 67–8. 'By the eighteenth
century, the influence of Roman Catholic Christianity had begun
its gradual spread among the people of western and southern Korea.
Catholicism was regarded a foreign creed that threatened the state;
by 1865 there were about 22,000 Catholics. The *tonghak* was a
peasant cult that reacted against this spread of Western teachings.'

4   UCLA International Institute, *Treaty of Annexation: Annexation
of Korea by Japan, August 22, 1910,* 10 December 2004, viewed
12 November 2017, <http://international.ucla.edu/institute/
article/18447>.

5   Yohei Kono, *Statement by the Chief Cabinet Secretary Yohei Kono
on the result of the study on the issue of 'comfort women',* Ministry of
Foreign Affairs of Japan, 4 August 1993, viewed 12 November
2017, <https://web.archive.org/web/20140709022903/http:/www.
mofa.go.jp/policy/women/fund/state9308.html>.

6   Bruce Cumings, *North Korea: Another Country,* The New Press,
New York, 2003, p. 116. 'Kim Il-sung was particularly popular
among the Koreans in Manchuria, it is said that there were many
Koreans who praised him as a local hero and gave him, secretly,
both spiritual and material support.'

7   Also known as Baekdu. Korea Konsult, *Mt Paektu – the birthplace
of Korean revolution,* viewed 12 November 2017, <http://www.
koreakonsult.com/Attraction_Paektu_eng.html>.

8   Franco Mazzei, 'Capire la Cina. Dalla geopolitica alla geocultura',
in Massimo Galluppi and Franco Mazzei (eds), *Campania e Cina,*
Esi, Naples, 2005.

9   This is the theoretical basis of the dichotomy between the
'government of man' (to which China and North Korea subscribe)
and 'government of law' (prevalent in the West).

10 Kim Jong-il, *Aphorism,* Foreign Language Publishing House,
Pyongyang, Juche 103, 2014.

11 Kim Jiyoon, Karl Friedoff, Kang Chungku and Lee Euicheol, *South
Korean Attitudes Toward North Korea and Reunification,* Asian Public
Opinion Report, The Asian Institute for Policy Studies, Seoul,
2015, viewed 24 November 2017, <https://thediplomat.com/

wp-content/uploads/2015/01/thediplomat_2015-01-29_13-53-09.
pdf>.

12 Hojunester, 'What is minjok?', blog, 1 December 2012,
viewed 24 November 2017, <https://hojunester.wordpress.
com/2012/12/01/what-is-korean-identity/>.

13 From Russian and Chinese racial and ideological prejudice
vis-à-vis Koreans stems the desperation for self-reliance. 'Is it any
wonder that for a Communist arrested by both Chinese and Soviet
comrades, independence and self-reliance would later become Kim
Il Sung's leitmotiv?' Cumings, *North Korea*, p. 118.

14 Rees, *Korea*.

15 Cumings, *North Korea*, p. 118: 'during the purges of the late
1930s Stalin executed every Korean agent of the Communist
International he could get his hands on'.

16 'From August 1945 until January 1946, the Soviets worked with
a coalition of communists and nationalists, led by a Christian
educator named Cho Man-sik.' Bruce Cumings, *Korea's Place in the
Sun: A Modern History*, updated edn, W. W. Norton, New York,
2005 [1997], p. 227.

17 Clearly, it is irrelevant who threw the first stone – whether the
North Korean troops invaded the South or if they were lured into
the conflict by provocations, as several historians have recently
claimed. Sooner or later the North and the South were going to
clash. Were the Allies aware of this reality? Absolutely not. And
did they care? Not at all. Even today, the average American knows
little or nothing about the Korean War, a conflict in which almost
40,000 American soldiers died (compared to the 58,000 who lost
their lives in Vietnam).

18 Richard Ernsberger Jr, 'Interview: Melinda Pash, Why is Korea
the "Forgotten War"?', *American History Magazine*, 31 March
2014, viewed 24 November 2017, <http://www.historynet.com/
interview-melinda-pash-why-is-korea-the-forgotten-war.htm>.

19 This was an infamous battalion for provoking incidents, such as
the one resulting in Japan's invasion of Manchuria in 1931. Many
believe that actors like Kim Sok-won provoked the North into the
conflict; indeed, from March to December 1949, several attacks
were launched from the South along the thirty-eighth parallel.

'The Korean cadets at the Academy spilt into two factions: a pro-Japanese faction led by Hong Sa Ik and Kim Suk Won, and an anti-Japanese faction led by Ji Chung Chun and Kim Gyong Chun. Col. Kim Suk Won was awarded numerous medals by Emperor Hirohito for his valor in China and went around Korea making speeches in support of the Emperor's war effort.' Kim Young Sik, 'Who were the Soviet Koreans? The left-right confrontation in Korea – its origin', *Association for Asian Research*, 11 May 2003, viewed 24 November 2017, <http://www.asianresearch.org/articles/1632.html>.

20 In Iraq, Shia militia, Iranian revolutionary guards, Turkish troops, Kurdish fighters, even warlords and armed groups were allowed to participate along with the predominantly Shia Iraqi army in the siege of Mosul. Once the city fell, Sunni boys and men streaming out of Mosul were stopped, searched, arrested and interrogated at checkpoints manned by these groups, and many of them simply vanished. Author interview with refugees from Mosul, October 2017.

21 *Interview with a Chinese Veteran from the Korean War,* YouTube, 22 April 2015, viewed 24 November 2017, <https://www.youtube.com/watch?v=oGrO4emyZG8>.

22 Cumings, *North Korea,* pp. 1, 4.

23 *North Korea Nuclear's Trump Card,* 7 October 2017, BBC Panorama, <http://www.bbc.co.uk/programmes/b097m386>.

24 Lincoln Riddle, 'The Korean War – a war of many names', *War History Online,* 16 June 2017, viewed 24 November 2017, <https://www.warhistoryonline.com/korean-war/10-top-facts-the-korean-war-m.html>.

25 'The war in Korea has already almost destroyed that nation of 20,000,000 people. I have never seen such devastation. I have seen, I guess, as much blood and disaster as any living man, and it just curdled my stomach...After I looked at that wreckage and those thousands of women and children and everything, I vomited... If you go on indefinitely, you are perpetuating a slaughter such as I have never heard of in the history of mankind.' Anthony B. Herbert and James T. Wooten, *Soldier,* Holt, Rinehart and Winston, New York, 1973.

26 Christine Ahn, 'The high costs of US warmongering against North Korea', *Truthout*, 26 April 2017, viewed 24 November 2017, <http://www.truth-out.org/news/item/40367-the-high-costs-of-us-warmongering-against-north-korea>.

27 Riddle, 'The Korean War – a war of many names', *War History Online*.

28 *Juche Strong,* 2013, Rob Montz, Vimeo, viewed 24 November, <https://vimeo.com/65907063>.

29 ibid.

30 Evan Osnos, 'The risk of nuclear war with North Korea', *The New Yorker*, 18 September 2017, viewed 24 November 2017, <https://www.newyorker.com/magazine/2017/09/18/the-risk-of-nuclear-war-with-north-korea>.

31 Tangun's parents were said to be Hwanung, the Son of Heaven, and a bear who had been transformed into a woman. Many subsequent kingdoms of Korea, such as Buyeo, Goguryeo, Balhae, Goryeo and Joseon worshipped the mountain.

32 Kim Jong-il, *Aphorism.*

33 The mountain is often referred to in slogans, such as 'Let us accomplish the Korean revolution in the revolutionary spirit of Baektu, the spirit of the blizzards of Baektu!' North Korean media even celebrates portentous natural phenomenon witnessed at the mountain.

34 L. Ron Hubbard, *Dianetics: The Modern Science of Mental Health,* Bridge Publications, Commerce City, CA, 2007 [1950].

35 Grace Lee, 'The political philosophy of juche', *Stanford Journal of East Asian Affairs*, vol. 3, no. 1, 2003, viewed 24 November 2017, <https://s3.amazonaws.com/berkley-center/030101LeePoliticalPhilosophyJuche.pdf>.

36 Ironically, Hwang Jang-yop, the man who was instrumental in putting together the ideology of *juche,* defected to South Korea in February 1997.

37 Anna Fifield, 'Life under Kim Jong Un', *The Washington Post*, 17 November 2017, viewed 24 November 2017, <https://www.washingtonpost.com/graphics/2017/world/north-korea-defectors/?utm_term=.8916b4d65737>.

38 *Juche Strong*, R. Montz.

39 Columbia Law School, 'Juche ideology', course materials, viewed
    24 November, <http://www2.law.columbia.edu/course_00S_
    L9436_001/North%20Korea%20materials/3.html>.

40 'The Kim family tree: a family firm', *TIME*, 2016, viewed
    24 November 2017, <http://content.time.com/time/
    interactive/0,31813,2107093,00.html>. Kim Jong-il was the eldest
    son from Kim Il-sung's marriage to his first wife. He had another
    son with her who died in an accident and three more with his
    second wife.

41 Fyodor Tertitskiy, 'Life in North Korea – the early years',
    The Guardian, 21 December 2015, viewed 24 November
    2017, <https://www.theguardian.com/world/2015/dec/21/
    life-in-north-korea-the-early-years#img-2>.

42 Robert Collins, *Marked for Life: Songbun. North Korea's Social
    Classification System*, The Committee for Human Rights in North
    Korea, Washington, DC, 2012, viewed 24 November 2017, <https://
    www.hrnk.org/uploads/pdfs/HRNK_Songbun_Web.pdf>.

43 In a seminal film, *Tale of Two Sisters,* about twin sisters born
    in North Korea, one ends up being raised in South Korea and
    the other in North Korea. The South Korean sister becomes a
    prostitute while the North Korean has a happy family life. Leaving
    North Korea is the biggest sin that anybody can commit. In
    Scientology, those who leave are considered fair game, enemies
    who must be stopped. According to the theory of the Immortal
    Socio-Political Body, North Korean dissidents lose their identity,
    they become limbs without a brain, a sort of existential zombie.

44 *Juche Strong*, R. Montz.

45 Steven Denney, 'North Korean nationalism: lessons from
    Pyongyang', *SinoNK*, 8 June 2016, viewed 24 November 2017,
    <http://sinonk.com/2016/06/08/north-korean-nationalism-lessons-
    from-pyongyang/>. Research conducted in 2013.

Chapter 2 – Broken Identity

1   Bruce Cumings, *North Korea: Another Country,* The New Press,
    New York, 2003, p. 119.

2   Kim Jiyoon, Karl Friedoff, Kang Chungku and Lee Euicheol, *South
    Korean Attitudes Toward North Korea and Reunification*, Asian Public

Opinion Report, The Asian Institute for Policy Studies, Seoul, 2015, viewed 24 November 2017, <https://thediplomat.com/wp-content/uploads/2015/01/thediplomat_2015-01-29_13-53-09.pdf>.

3   Steven Denney, 'North Korean nationalism: lessons from Pyongyang', *SinoNK*, 8 June 2016, viewed 24 November 2017, <http://sinonk.com/2016/06/08/north-korean-nationalism-lessons-from-pyongyang/>.

4   Kim Hyung-A, *Korea's Development Under Park Chung Hee: Rapid Industrialization, 1961–79*, RoutledgeCurzon, London and New York, 2004.

5   ibid.

6   John F. Kennedy, 'Joint statement following discussions with chairman Chung Hee Park of Korea', 14 November 1961, online by Gerhard Peters and John T. Woolley, *The American Presidency Project*, viewed 24 November 2017, <http://www.presidency.ucsb.edu/ws/?pid=8442>. 'Chairman Park and President Kennedy concluded today a friendly and constructive exchange of views on the current situation in Korea and the Far East and the various matters of interest to the governments and peoples of the Republic of Korea and the United States of America...The two leaders reaffirmed the strong bonds of friendship traditionally existing between the two countries and their determination to intensify their common efforts toward the establishment of world peace based on freedom and justice.'

7   'Import substitution industrialisation (ISI) is a trade and economic policy which advocates replacing foreign imports with domestic production. ISI is based on the premise that a country should attempt to reduce its foreign dependency through the local production of industrialised products.' 'Import substitution industrialization', *Wikipedia,* 12 November 2017, viewed 24 November 2017, <https://en.wikipedia.org/wiki/Import_substitution_industrialization>.

8   Jorge I. Dominguez, 'The perfect dictatorship? Comparing authoritarian rule in South Korea and in Argentina, Brazil, Chile, and Mexico', presented at the Annual Meeting of the American Political Science Association, Boston, 29 August – 1 September

2002, viewed 24 November 2017, <https://wcfia.harvard.edu/files/wcfia/files/690_theperfectdictatorship.pdf>.

9   Donald Gregg, 'Park Chung Hee', *TIME*, 23 August 1999, viewed 24 November 2017, <http://content.time.com/time/world/article/0,8599,2054405,00.html>.

10 ibid.

11 ibid.

12 Cumings, *North Korea,* p. 186.

13 Christine Ahn, 'The high costs of US warmongering against North Korea', *Truthout*, 26 April 2017, viewed 24 November 2017, <http://www.truth-out.org/news/item/40367-the-high-costs-of-us-warmongering-against-north-korea>.

14 *Inside North Korea*, part 2/3, 19 December 2011, VICE Travel, viewed 24 November 2017, <https://www.youtube.com/watch?annotation_id=annotation_448028&feature=iv&index=2&list=PL10943F1A08C72A17&src_vid=24R8JObNNQ4&v=xw46Ll-Zy4s>.

15 *North Korea's Dangerous Border: Inside The DMZ [Pt.1]*, Dena Takruri, 12 September 2017, viewed 24 November 2017, <https://www.youtube.com/watch?v=a12yniZVGLQ>.

16 Author interview with Urs Gerber, October 2017.

17 Lisa Brady, 'How wildlife is thriving in the Korean Peninsula's demilitarised zone', *The Guardian*, 13 April 2012, viewed 24 November 2017, <https://www.theguardian.com/environment/2012/apr/13/wildlife-thriving-korean-demilitarised-zone>.

18 Rowena Ryan, 'The mysterious fake town on North Korea's border', *News.com.au*, 11 July 2014, viewed 24 November 2017, <http://nypost.com/2014/07/11/the-mysterious-fake-town-on-north-koreas-border/>.

19 *North Korea's Dangerous Border: Inside The DMZ [Pt.1]*, D. Takruri.

20 The Economist, 'Miscalculating the cost of unification', *Business Insider*, 7 December 2014, viewed 24 November 2017, <http://uk.businessinsider.com/miscalculating-the-cost-of-unification-2014-12>.

21 Yuka Koshino, 'Q&A: how much do US military bases in Japan and Korea cost?', *The Wall Street Journal*, 28 April

2016, viewed 24 November 2017, <https://www.wsj.com/articles/q-a-how-much-do-u-s-military-bases-in-japan-and-korea-cost-1461822624>.

22 'North Korea: "no apology" for S Korea Cheonan sinking', *BBC News*, 24 March 2015, viewed 24 November 2017, <http://www.bbc.co.uk/news/world-asia-32013750>.

23 John Dower, *Embracing Defeat,* Penguin Press, London, 1999, pp. 525–6.

24 ibid., pp. 540–1.

25 ibid., pp. 525–6.

26 ibid., p. 541.

27 ibid.

28 ibid.

29 Aaron Forsberg, *America and the Japanese Miracle*, University of North Carolina Press, London, 2000.

30 John Dower, *Embracing Defeat*.

Chapter 3 – Survival Economy

1 Loretta Napoleoni, 'The Chinese Miracle: A Modern Day Industrial Revolution', The European Financial Review, 12 February 2012, viewed 12 December 2017, <http://www.europeanfinancialreview.com/?p=2101>.

2 Anita Chan, *China's Workers Under Assault: Exploitation and Abuse in a Globalizing Economy,* Routledge, Abingdon and New York, 2015 [2001], pp. 56–9. In March 1995, for example, the Chinese press reported that the manager of the South Korean Zhuhai Ruijin Electrical Goods Company in Guangdong had forced its 120 workers to kneel on the ground because, during the ten-minute break allowed them, they had failed to leave the workplace in groups of four, as prescribed by the factory's rules. This type of humiliation was common during the industrialisation of South Korea.

3 Franco Mazzei and Vittorio Volpi, *Asia al Centro* [Asia at the Center], Egea-Università Bocconi Editore, Milan, 2006, p. 155.

4 Manuel Castells, *End of Millennium*, 2nd edn, Blackwell Publishers, Oxford, 2000, pp. 270–1. See also Martin Jacques, *When China Rules the World,* Allen Lane, London, 2009.

5   Byung-Yeon Kim, *Unveiling the North Korean Economy: Collapse and Transition,* Cambridge University Press, Cambridge, 2017, p. 57.

6   Speech by President Ronald Reagan to the National Association of Evangelicals in Orlando, Florida, 8 March 1983, *Voices of Democracy: The US Oratory Project,* viewed 27 November 2017, <http://voicesofdemocracy.umd.edu/reagan-evil-empire-speech-text/>.

7   Kim, *Unveiling the North Korean Economy.*

8   Jun He and Jianchu Xu, 'Is there decentralization in North Korea? Evidence and lessons from the sloping land management program 2004–2014', *Land Use Policy,* vol. 61, 2017, pp. 113–25, <http://dx.doi.org/10.1016/j.landusepol.2016.11.020>.

9   J. Katona-Apte and A. Mokdad, 'Malnutrition of children in the Democratic People's Republic of North Korea', *Journal of Nutrition,* vol. 128, no. 8, 1998, pp. 1315–19.

10   He and Xu, 'Is there decentralization in North Korea?'

11   Kim, *Unveiling the North Korean Economy,* p. 50.

12   Interview with Kang Myung Do in *Money & Power in North Korea: The Hidden Economy,* 2015, video, NHK Documentary, viewed 27 November 2017, <https://www.youtube.com/watch?v=pKYBu9xIfac>.

13   *Money & Power in North Korea.*

14   ibid.

15   ibid.

16   ibid.

17   Kim, *Unveiling the North Korean Economy,* p. 160.

18   'How did the North Korean upper class get so many dollars?', 20 August 2014 (24), viewed 17 November 2017 <http://blog.donga.com/nambukstory/archives/88013>. Translated by the author.

19   ibid.

20   Han Jong-Woo and Jung Tae-Hern (eds), *Understanding North Korea: Indigenous Perspectives,* Lexington Books, Lanham, MD, 2014, p. 69.

21   S. Haggard, E. Jung and A. Melton, 'Is China subsidizing the DPRK? Part one: food', Peterson Institute for International Economics, 29 May 2013, viewed 23 November 2017, <http://blogs.piie.com/nk/?p=10488>.

22 'How did the North Korean upper class get so many dollars?'

23 Haggard et al., 'Is China subsidizing the DPRK?'

24 Tania Branigan, 'Kim Jong-un's uncle Jang Song-thaek executed, say North Korean state media', *The Guardian*, 12 December 2013, viewed 27 November 2017, <https://www.theguardian.com/world/2013/dec/12/north-korea-jang-song-thaek-executed>.

25 Evan Osnos, 'The risk of nuclear war with North Korea', *The New Yorker*, 18 September 2017, viewed 24 November 2017, <https://www.newyorker.com/magazine/2017/09/18/the-risk-of-nuclear-war-with-north-korea>.

26 Robert Collins, *Marked for Life: Songbun. North Korea's Social Classification System*, The Committee for Human Rights in North Korea, Washington, DC, 2012, viewed 24 November 2017, <https://www.hrnk.org/uploads/pdfs/HRNK_Songbun_Web.pdf>.

27 Human Rights Watch, 'North Korea: events of 2016', 2017, viewed 24 November 2017, <https://www.hrw.org/world-report/2017/country-chapters/north-korea>.

28 Anna Fifield, 'Life under Kim Jong Un', *The Washington Post*, 17 November 2017, viewed 24 November 2017, <https://www.washingtonpost.com/graphics/2017/world/north-korea-defectors/?utm_term=.8916b4d65737>.

29 Daniel Tudor and James Pearson, *North Korea Confidential: Private Markets, Fashion Trends, Prison Camps, Dissenters and Defectors*, Tuttle Publishing, North Clarendon, VT, 2015, p. 116.

30 ibid., p. 117.

31 Cited in Human Rights Watch, 'North Korea: events of 2016'.

32 ibid.

33 Fifield, 'Life under Kim Jong Un'.

34 Osnos, 'The risk of nuclear war with North Korea'. The New York channel is 'an office inside North Korea's mission to the United Nations, to handle the unavoidable parts of our nonexistent relationship. The office has, among other things, negotiated the release of prisoners and held informal talks about nuclear tensions.'

Chapter 4 – Status Quo: The Korean Model of Development

1   Several Western diplomats who reside in North Korea confirm that they socialise with North Koreans and have been in their homes many times. YouTube features plenty of amateur videos showing foreigners' interactions with ordinary North Koreans. For example, *North Korea Uncloaked: The Movie*, 2012, C.K. Media Enterprises, video, viewed 24 November 2017, <https://www.youtube.com/watch?v=czK6dSRIxZs&list=UUrAPOIeEk_BPcFdpWIDM7dg&index=5>; *North Korea Day 5*, 3 August 2016, video, Fun for Louis, viewed 27 November 2017, <https://www.youtube.com/watch?v=efqRUmazxBU&index=5&list=PLKdBO8TXUFBgaqcNCd8xyokjUFEdUu9LU>.

2   Ting Shi and David Tweed, 'China and Russia warn the US not to seek North Korean regime change', *Bloomberg Politics*, 12 September 2017, viewed 24 November 2017, <https://www.bloomberg.com/news/articles/2017-09-12/in-sanctioning-kim-china-and-russia-warn-u-s-no-regime-change>.

3   Byung-Yeon Kim, *Unveiling the North Korean Economy: Collapse and Transition,* Cambridge University Press, Cambridge, 2017.

4   'The major success in this regard has been the strengthening of the Integrated Management of Neonatal and Childhood Illnesses (IMNCI), and the sharp increase in immunization coverage from 43 per cent in 1998 to 96 per cent in 2016. [...] Estimates of the Maternal Mortality Ratio (MMR) have declined from roughly 97 deaths per 100,000 live births in 1990, to 66 per 100,000 in 2014. Ninety-two per cent of births occur in hospitals and eight per cent at home.' The Bassiouni Group, *Situation Analysis of Children and Women in the Democratic People's Republic of Korea – 2017*, United Nations Children's Fund, Pyongyang, 2016, viewed 24 November 2017, <https://www.unicef.org/dprk/Situation_Analysis_of_Children_and_Women_in_DPR_Korea_UNICEF_2017.pdf>.

5   *Counting the Cost: N Korea unfazed by talks of increasing sanctions,* Al Jazeera English, 9 September 2017, viewed 24 November 2017, <https://www.youtube.com/watch?v=RCZo-muQuso>.

6   ibid.

7   ibid.

8   Frank Ruediger, 'Economic sanctions and the nuclear issue: lessons from North Korean trade', *38North*, 18 September 2017, viewed 24 November 2017, <http://www.38north.org/2017/09/rfrank091817/>.

9   Anna Fifield, 'Life under Kim Jong Un', *The Washington Post*, 17 November 2017, viewed 24 November 2017, <https://www.washingtonpost.com/graphics/2017/world/north-korea-defectors/?utm_term=.8916b4d65737>.

10 Fifield, 'Life under Kim Jong Un'.

11 *Money & Power in North Korea: The Hidden Economy,* 2015, NHK Documentary, viewed 24 November 2017, <https://www.youtube.com/watch?v=pKYBu9xIfac>.

12 ibid.

13 Fifield, 'Life under Kim Jong Un'.

14 *North Korean Labor Camps: Part 1 of 7*, 19 December 2011, video, VICE News, viewed 24 November 2017, <https://www.youtube.com/watch?v=awQDLoOnkdI>.

15 Franz-Stefan Gady, 'Is North Korea fighting for Assad in Syria?', *The Diplomat,* 24 March 2016, viewed 9 November 2017, <https://thediplomat.com/2016/03/is-north-korea-fighting-for-assad-in-syria/>. 'North Korea has a history of boots on the ground in Syria. For example, Pyongyang sent 25 pilots to Syria during the Arab-Israeli War of 1967, 30 pilots during the 1973 Arab-Israeli (to both Syria and Egypt), and 40 pilots and 75 air force instructors in 1975 and 1976. The Korean pilots provided training and in some instances even flew combat missions against Israel. During the 1980s, North Korea dispatched special operations forces to Syria to help train the conventional Syrian Arab Army and its allies in insurgency tactics. "In 1984–1986 and 1990, 50 and 30 North Korean military instructors were sent to Syria, respectively," the US–Korea Institute analysis elaborates. North Korean soldiers allegedly also operated 122 millimeter truck-mounted multiple rocket launchers (the weapon systems were supplied by Pyongyang) during the 1982 Islamic uprising in the city of Hama. Up to 25,000 civilians were killed when Syrian government forces suppressed the uprising by indiscriminately shelling the city with artillery. One of the key facilitators in the early stages of the civil

purportedly was the late Chief of the Korea's People's Army Staff, General Kim Kyok Sik. Beginning in the 1970s, he served for over a decade as Pyongyang's military attaché in Damascus.'

16 *This Is What It's Like Inside North Korea's Luxury Ski Resort | Short Film Showcase,* video, National Geographic, 2017, viewed 24 November 2017, <https://www.youtube.com/watch?v=csoP8Didoi0>. Over the last two winter seasons, North Koreans have usually been granted a ski excursion by their factories or institutions and they go to the resort in large groups by coaches.

17 *N Korea unfazed by talks of increasing sanctions,* Al Jazeera English.

18 Kim, *Unveiling the North Korean Economy: Collapse and Transition,* p. 119.

19 Bryan Harris, 'Unveiling the North Korean economy, by Byung-Yeon Kim', *Financial Times,* 4 September 2017, viewed 27 November 2017, <https://www.ft.com/content/2de06fec-8d6a-11e7-9084-d0c17942ba93>.

20 Kim, *Unveiling the North Korean Economy,* p. 119.

21 Fifield, 'Life under Kim Jong Un'.

22 ibid. Notels are 'small DVD players with screens'.

23 Evan Osnos, 'The risk of nuclear war with North Korea', *The New Yorker,* 18 September 2017, viewed 24 November 2017, <https://www.newyorker.com/magazine/2017/09/18/the-risk-of-nuclear-war-with-north-korea>.

24 Osnos, 'The risk of nuclear war with North Korea'.

25 *The Happiest People on Earth. North Korea: Rulers, Citizens, and Official Narrative,* 2 July 2017, video, RT, viewed 24 November 2017, <https://www.youtube.com/watch?v=7ZMB_TxyuNM>.

26 Daniel Tudor, *A Geek in Korea: Discovering Asia's New Kingdom of Cool,* Tuttle Publishing, North Clarendon, VT, 2014.

27 Jonathan Corrado, 'Putting myths to bed: a review of "North Korea Confidential"', *DailyNK,* 11 March 2015, viewed 24 November 2017, <http://www.dailynk.com/english/read.php?cataId=nk02501&num=12966>.

28 Human Rights Watch, 'North Korea: events of 2016', 2017, viewed 24 November 2017, <https://www.hrw.org/world-report/2017/country-chapters/north-korea>.

29 ibid.

30 Osnos, 'The risk of nuclear war with North Korea'.

31 *The Happiest People on Earth.*

32 Maya Oppenheim, 'What it's like to be a teenager in North Korea', *Independent*, 9 September 2016, viewed 24 November 2017, <http://www.independent.co.uk/news/people/north-korea-independence-day-dating-love-sex-drinking-video-games-and-being-gay-in-north-korea-life-a7233526.html>.

33 Author interview with a North Korean defector, August 2017.

34 Rose Kwak, 'What do North Koreans do for fun?', *Korea Economic Institute of America*, 2017, viewed 24 November 2017, <http://keia.org/what-do-north-koreans-do-fun>.

35 Noelle Mateer, 'A rare look inside everyday North Korea', *That's Shanghai,* 28 October 2015, viewed 24 November 2017, <http://www.thatsmags.com/shanghai/post/11417/lit-fest-everyday-north-korea>.

36 Fifield, 'Life under Kim Jong Un'.

Chapter 5 – Cyber Scapegoat

1   Eric Talmadge, 'North Korea, cyberattacks and "Lazarus": what we really know', *Phys.org,* 2 June 2017, viewed 9 November 2017, <https://phys.org/news/2017-06-north-korea-cyberattacks-lazarus.html>.

2   David E. Sanger and Martin Fackler, 'NSA breached North Korean networks before Sony attack, officials say', *The New York Times*, 18 January 2015, viewed 24 November 2017, <https://www.nytimes.com/2015/01/19/world/asia/nsa-tapped-into-north-korean-networks-before-sony-attack-officials-say.html?_r=1>.

3   Jenny Jun, Scott LaFoy and Ethan Sohn, *North Korea's Cyber Operations: Strategy and Responses*, Center for Strategic International Studies, Washington, DC, 2015, viewed 27 November 2017, <https://csis-prod.s3.amazonaws.com/s3fs-public/legacy_files/files/publication/151216_Cha_NorthKoreasCyberOperations_Web.pdf>, p. 28.

4   Sanger and Fackler, 'NSA breached North Korean networks before Sony attack'.

5 Ju-min Park and James Pearson, 'In North Korea, hackers are a handpicked, pampered elite', *Reuters*, 5 December 2014, viewed 24 November 2017, <http://uk.reuters.com/article/us-sony-cybersecurity-northkorea/in-north-korea-hackers-are-a-handpicked-pampered-elite-idUSKCN0JJ08B20141205>.

6 ibid.

7 Sanger and Fackler, 'NSA breached North Korean networks before Sony attack'.

8 Talmadge, 'North Korea, cyberattacks and "Lazarus"'.

9 Park and Pearson, 'In North Korea, hackers are a handpicked, pampered elite'.

10 James Waterhouse and Anna Doble, 'Bureau 121: North Korea's elite hackers and a "tasteful" hotel in China', *BBC*, 29 May 2015, viewed 24 November 2017, <http://www.bbc.co.uk/newsbeat/article/32926248/bureau-121-north-koreas-elite-hackers-and-a-tasteful-hotel-in-china>.

11 AFP, 'South Korea sounds alert after official websites hacked', *Security Week*, 25 June 2013, viewed 24 November 2017, <http://www.securityweek.com/south-korea-sounds-alert-after-official-websites-hacked>.

12 Brian Prince, 'South Korea cyber attack tied to DarkSeoul crew: Symantec', *Security Week*, 27 June 2013, viewed 24 November 2017, <http://www.securityweek.com/south-korea-cyber-attack-tied-darkseoul-crew-symantec>.

13 Choe Sang-Hun, 'Computer networks in South Korea are paralyzed in cyberattacks', *The New York Times*, 20 March 2013, viewed 24 November 2017, <http://www.nytimes.com/2013/03/21/world/asia/south-korea-computer-network-crashes.html>.

14 ibid.

15 'The Interview: a guide to the cyber attack on Hollywood', *BBC*, 29 December 2014, viewed 24 November 2017, <http://www.bbc.co.uk/news/entertainment-arts-30512032>.

16 Dann Albright, '2014's final controversy: Sony hack, The Interview, and North Korea', *MakeUseOf.com*, 3 January 2015, viewed 24 November 2017, <http://www.makeuseof.com/tag/sony-hack-the-interview-north-korea/>.

17 'The Interview: a guide to the cyber attack on Hollywood'.

18 'Sony hacking scandal: execs convinced it's an inside job', *TMZ*, 17 December 2014, viewed 24 November 2017, <http://www.tmz.com/2014/12/17/sony-hack-inside-job-north-korea-investigation/>.

19 *Sony Hacking Scandal – Crime of the Year*, 18 December 2014, video, TheLipTV, viewed 24 November 2017, <https://www.youtube.com/watch?v=QlKNoZu-UKA>.

20 Bruce Schneier, 'More data on attributing the Sony attack', *Schneier on Security*, 31 December 2014, viewed 24 November 2017, <https://www.schneier.com/blog/archives/2014/12/more_data_on_at.html>.

21 Marc Rogers, 'The Sony saga: 10 reasons why the FBI is wrong', *ITProPortal*, 22 December 2014, viewed 24 November 2017, <https://www.itproportal.com/2014/12/22/10-pieces-evidence-suggest-sony-pictures-hack-done-north-korea/>.

22 Alex Hern and Samuel Gibbs, 'What is WannaCry ransomware and why is it attacking global computers?', *The Guardian*, 12 May 2017, viewed 24 November 2017, <https://www.theguardian.com/technology/2017/may/12/nhs-ransomware-cyber-attack-what-is-wanacrypt0r-20>. The WannaCry ransomware cryptoworm was used in a worldwide cyberattack in May 2017 that targeted computers running the Microsoft Windows operating system by encrypting data and demanding ransom payments in the Bitcoin cryptocurrency.

23 Talmadge, 'North Korea, cyberattacks and "Lazarus"'.

24 ibid.

25 ibid.

26 For further explanation see 'Blockchain', *Wikipedia*, 25 November 2017, viewed 27 November 2017, <https://en.wikipedia.org/wiki/Blockchain>.

27 Chrisee Dela Paz, 'Timeline: tracing the $81-million stolen fund from Bangladesh Bank', *Rappler*, 17 March 2016, viewed 24 November 2017, <https://www.rappler.com/business/industries/209-banking-and-financial-services/125999-timeline-money-laundering-bangladesh-bank>.

28 Serajul Quardir, 'Bangladesh Bank exposed hackers by cheap switches, no firewall: police', *Reuters*, 21 April 2016, viewed 24 November 2017, <https://www.reuters.com/article/us-usa-fed-bangladesh/bangladesh-bank-exposed-to-hackers-by-cheap-switches-no-firewall-police-idUSKCN0XI1UO>.

29 Krishna Das and Jonathan Spicer, 'The SWIFT hack: how the New York Fed fumbled over the Bangladesh Bank cyber-heist', *Reuters*, 21 July 2016, viewed 24 November 2017, <http://www.reuters.com/investigates/special-report/cyber-heist-federal/>.

30 Sherisse Pham, 'Russia just gave North Korea's internet a big boost', *CNN Tech*, 2 October 2017, viewed 24 November 2017, <http://money.cnn.com/2017/10/02/technology/north-korea-russia-internet-link/index.html>.

31 Author interview with Nirjhar Mazumder, September 2017.

32 Arun Devnath and Michael Riley, 'Bangladesh Bank heist probe said to find three hacker groups', *Bloomberg Technology*, 10 May 2016, viewed 24 November 2017, <https://www.bloomberg.com/news/articles/2016-05-10/bangladesh-bank-heist-probe-said-to-find-three-groups-of-hackers>.

33 'Missing IT expert Zoha back home', *The Daily Star,* 24 March 2016, viewed 24 November 2017, <http://www.thedailystar.net/frontpage/missing-it-expert-zoha-back-home-1198780>.

34 Bangladeshi blogger Nirjhar Mazumder interview with Tanvir Hassan Zoha, October 2017.

35 Habibullah Mizan, '13 BB staff guilty of negligence, says CID', *the independent*, 27 August 2016, viewed 24 November 2017, <http://www.theindependentbd.com/printversion/details/57699>. Among the thirteen Bangladesh Bank officials, four were from the accounts and budget department, three from information technology operations and communications, two from forex reserves and treasury management, and four from the payment systems department.

36 Nirjhar Mazumder interview with Tanvir Hassan Zoha, October 2017.

Chapter 6 – The Last Evil Standing

1   Adrian Levy and Catherine Scott-Clark, *Deception: Pakistan, the United States, and the Secret Trade in Nuclear Weapons*, Walker, New York, 2007.

2   David Sanger, 'Threats and responses: alliances; in North Korea and Pakistan, deep roots of nuclear barter', *The New York Times*, 24 November 2002, viewed 24 November 2017, <http://www.nytimes.com/2002/11/24/world/threats-responses-alliances-north-korea-pakistan-deep-roots-nuclear-barter.html>.

3   *Why is North Korea in the Axis of Evil?* Annabel Park interview with John Feffer, 18 January 2007, video, Eric Byler, viewed 24 November 2017, <https://www.youtube.com/watch?v=IEBlFkqIdCo>.

4   Levy and Scott-Clark, *Deception*, p. 124.

5   *Who Made North Korea a Nuclear Power: Dr A.Q. Khan, or Pakistan?* 17 May 2017, video, Global Conflict, viewed 24 November 2017, <https://www.youtube.com/watch?v=B7ehXxA5oj4&t=135s>.

6   Bill Powell and Tim McGirk, 'The man who sold the bomb', *TIME*, 6 February 2005, viewed 24 November 2017, <content.time.com/time/magazine/article/0,9171,1025193,00.html>.

7   Samuel Ramani, 'The long history of the Pakistan–North Korea nexus', *The Diplomat*, 30 August 2016, viewed 24 November 2017, <https://thediplomat.com/2016/08/the-long-history-of-the-pakistan-north-korea-nexus/>.

8   *Who Made North Korea a Nuclear Power: Dr A.Q. Khan, or Pakistan?*

9   Don Oberdorfer, *The Two Koreas: A Contemporary History*, Basic Books, New York, 2001 [1997].

10 David E. Sanger and William J. Broad, 'Trump inherits a secret cyberwar against North Korean missiles', *The New York Times*, 4 March 2017, viewed 10 November 2017, <https://www.nytimes.com/2017/03/04/world/asia/north-korea-missile-program-sabotage.html?_r=0>; Christine Ahn, 'War is not an option for Korea', *Foreign Policy in Focus*, 18 March 2017, viewed 27 November 2017, <http://fpif.org/war-is-not-an-option-for-korea/>.

11 *Putin: North Koreans Would Rather Eat Grass Than Give Up Nukes, If They Don't Feel Safe*, 6 September 2017, video, Russia

Insider, viewed 24 November 2017, <https://www.youtube.com/watch?v=xFedyqandWU>.

12 *Why North Korea Wants Nuclear Weapons*, 24 April 2017, video, Caspian Report, viewed 24 November 2017, <https://www.youtube.com/watch?v=ykYRsmIQkyw>.

13 Launched in 2003, the Six-Party Talks are aimed at ending North Korea's nuclear program through negotiations involving China, the United States, North and South Korea, Japan and Russia. J. Bajoria and B. Xu, 'The six party talks on North Korea's nuclear program', *Council on Foreign Relations*, 30 September 2013, viewed 10 November 2017, <https://www.cfr.org/backgrounder/six-party-talks-north-koreas-nuclear-program>.

14 John Feffer and John Gershman, 'Fearful symmetry: Washington and Pyongyang', *Institute for Policy Studies*, 1 July 2003, viewed 10 November 2017, <https://www.ips-dc.org/fearful_symmetry_washington_and_pyongyang/>.

15 Seymour M. Hersh, 'The cold test', *The New Yorker*, 27 January 2003, viewed 10 November 2017, <https://www.newyorker.com/magazine/2003/01/27/the-cold-test>.

16 *North Korea Nuclear's Trump Card*, 7 October 2017, BBC Panorama, <http://www.bbc.co.uk/programmes/b097m386>.

17 ibid.

18 ibid.

19 AP, 'Less than one aircraft carrier? the cost of North Korea's nukes', *CNBC*, 20 July 2017, viewed 24 November 2017, <https://www.cnbc.com/2017/07/20/less-than-one-aircraft-carrier-the-cost-of-north-koreas-nukes.html>.

20 ibid.

Appendix C – South Korea Timeline

1 'South Korea – timeline', *BBC*, 11 May 2017, viewed 27 November 2017, <http://www.bbc.com/news/world-asia-pacific-15292674>; 'South Korea history timeline', *World Atlas*, 7 April 2017, viewed 27 November 2017, <http://www.worldatlas.com/webimage/countrys/asia/southkorea/krtimeln.htm>.

Glossary

Bureau 121. North Korea's de facto cyberwarfare agency consisting of the state's most talented hackers. Created in 1998, it is part of the Reconnaissance General Bureau, North Korea's primary intelligence agency.

Byungjin line. Known as 'parallel development', the *byungjin* line is a series of policies adopted by Kim Jong-un that stress the simultaneous development of the national economy and nuclear weapons program.

Chaju. The drive for political and ideological independence, especially from the Soviet Union and China. It is one of the three fundamental principles of the *juche* ideology.

Charip. The need for economic self-reliance and self-sufficiency, one of the fundamental principles of the *juche* ideology.

Chawi. The need for military independence through a viable national defence system.

Cho Man-sik. A nationalist activist in the Koreas' independence movement against the Japanese.

Choson. The dynastic kingdom of Korea that spanned from 1392 to 1897, losing influence in the nineteenth century amid foreign pressures.

Donju. A growing class of entrepreneurial elites known as the 'masters of money'. They specialise in importing consumer goods from China, selling them at a profit in the unofficial North Korean economy.

Eumjugamu. Literally translates to 'music, dance and drink' and is deeply rooted in the entertainment of both North and South Koreans, going back to the times of ancient Korean festivals.

Gyohwaso. Known as 'correctional re-education centres', these labour camps are reserved for criminals convicted of serious crimes or minor political infractions.

Jangmadang. Technically illegal, but tolerated unofficial markets that constitute the backbone of the informal North Korean economy.

Jang Sung-taek. Uncle of Kim Jong-un and member of the Politburo, Jang was executed in 2013 for charges of corruption and conspiracy to commit treason. Many have viewed his demise as evidence of Kim's further consolidation of power within his own circle.

Juche. The official state doctrine of North Korea, roughly translating to 'self-reliance'.

Kim Jong-nam. Brother of Kim Jong-un and eldest son of Kim Jong-il. He was assassinated by chemical agents in 2017 in Kuala Lumpur International Airport, likely due to his criticism of the family regime.

Kwanliso. Political prison camps operated by North Korea's National Security Agency. They are estimated to house between 80,000 and 120,000 prisoners.

Manchukuo. The puppet-state of the empire of Japan following the annexation of Manchuria in 1932.

Man'gyongdae Revolutionary School. Established in 1947 by Kim Il-sung under the original name 'The School for the Offspring of Revolutionary Martyrs', Man'gyongdae was a boarding school for orphans following the aftermath of the Korean War. The school would later become the incubator of some of the top-ranking members of the DPRK.

Minjok. A group of people who share a common history, ancestry and religion. They often reside in the same place and speak the same language.

Mt Paektu. Also known as Mt Baektu, Mount Paektu is the highest mountain in North Korea and in northern China and is an active volcano. It is a sacred place for people living on both sides of the 38th parallel because, according to Korean mythology, it was the birthplace of Tangun, the founder of the first Korean kingdom, Gojoseon (2333–108 BC).

Nongtaegi. Home-made moonshine commonly produced in the North Korean countryside.

Noraebang. Karaoke – actively frequented by North and South Koreans alike.

Paektu hyultong. North Koreans often use this expression, the 'Paektu bloodline', to describe Kim Jong-un's legitimacy as their leader.

Panmunjeom. Located in the Demilitarised Zone, 50 km north of Seoul and 10 km east from the city of Gaeseong, a city which now belongs to North Korea. This area is most notably known for being the location in which the armistice agreement was signed in 1953.

Park Chung-hee. President of South Korea from 1963 until his assassination in 1979. A controversial head of state, Park is credited for guiding South Korea towards its 'economic miracle', but also criticised for enforcing strict authoritarian measures in an effort to consolidate political power during his tenure.

Ren. One of the Confucian precepts, *ren* defines the individual, who exists only in relation to the other. In Chinese *ren* is also used as synonym of person, individual.

Rodong danryondae. Forced labour detention facilities designed for criminals convicted of petty crimes. Inmates spend half a day working and the remaining time being rewired to the system through propaganda.

Royal court economy. Separate from the public economy, the royal court economy is a secret fund established by Kim Jong-il that became the financial foundation of the Kim dynasty. These funds are mostly embezzled from the public and have been used for gifts to the elite, often without the party's approval.

Songbun. The caste system of North Korea based on the political, social and economic background of one's ancestors as well as their present social conduct. A person's position within the *songbun* determines their opportunities for employment, education and even food.

Suryong. The leader and indisputable leader of the *juche* doctrine. This title is reserved strictly for the Kim dynasty.

Waku. A licence to export and import goods.

Yangban. Dynastic aristocratic land owners who enjoyed exclusive access to politics.

Yeonjwaje. Known as 'guilt by association', up to three generations are considered equally culpable for crimes committed by a single member of the family. Those detained are commonly gathered along with their families.

Bibliography

Primary sources

Author interviews, August–October 2017.

Secondary sources

Articles, blogs and news reports
AFP, 'South Korea sounds alert after official websites hacked', *Security Week*, 25 June 2013, viewed 24 November 2017, <http://www.securityweek.com/south-korea-sounds-alert-after-official-websites-hacked>.

Albright, Dann, '2014's final controversy: Sony hack, The Interview, and North Korea', *MakeUseOf.com*, 3 January 2015, viewed 24 November 2017, <http://www.makeuseof.com/tag/sony-hack-the-interview-north-korea/>.

Ahn, Christine, 'War is not an option for Korea', *Foreign Policy in Focus,* 18 March 2017, viewed 27 November 2017, <http://fpif.org/war-is-not-an-option-for-korea/>.

Ahn, Christine, 'The high costs of US warmongering against North Korea', *Truthout*, 26 April 2017, viewed 24 November 2017, <http://www.truth-out.org/news/item/40367-the-high-costs-of-us-warmongering-against-north-korea>.

AP, 'Less than one aircraft carrier? the cost of North Korea's nukes', *CNBC*, 20 July 2017, viewed 24 November 2017, <https://

www.cnbc.com/2017/07/20/less-than-one-aircraft-carrier-the-cost-of-north-koreas-nukes.html>.

Bajoria, J. and Xu, B., 'The six party talks on North Korea's nuclear program', *Council on Foreign Relations*, 30 September 2013, viewed 10 November 2017, <https://www.cfr.org/backgrounder/six-party-talks-north-koreas-nuclear-program>.

Borger, Julian, 'Missile crisis by candlelight: Donald Trump's use of Mar-a-Lago raises security questions', *The Guardian*, 14 February 2017, viewed 12 November 2017, <https://www.theguardian.com/us-news/2017/feb/13/mar-a-lago-north-korea-missile-crisis-trump-national-security>.

Brady, Lisa, 'How wildlife is thriving in the Korean Peninsula's demilitarised zone', *The Guardian*, 13 April 2012, viewed 24 November 2017, <https://www.theguardian.com/environment/2012/apr/13/wildlife-thriving-korean-demilitarised-zone>.

Branigan, Tania, 'Kim Jong-un's uncle Jang Song-thaek executed, say North Korean state media', *The Guardian*, 12 December 2013, viewed 27 November 2017, <https://www.theguardian.com/world/2013/dec/12/north-korea-jang-song-thaek-executed>.

The British Museum, *Reginald Campbell Thompson (Biographical Details)*, viewed 12 November 2017, <http://www.britishmuseum.org/research/search_the_collection_database/term_details.aspx?bioId=93633>.

Choe Sang-Hun, 'Computer networks in South Korea are paralyzed in cyberattacks', *The New York Times*, 20 March 2013, viewed 24 November 2017, <http://www.nytimes.com/2013/03/21/world/asia/south-korea-computer-network-crashes.html>.

Choe Sang-Hun, 'US antimissile system goes live in South Korea', *The New York Times*, 2 May 2017, viewed 12 November 2017,

<https://www.nytimes.com/2017/05/02/world/asia/thaad-north-korea-missile-defense-us.html>.

Columbia Law School, 'Juche ideology', course materials, viewed 24 November, <http://www2.law.columbia.edu/course_00S_L9436_001/North%20Korea%20materials/3.html>.

Corrado, Jonathan, 'Putting myths to bed: a review of "North Korea Confidential"', *DailyNK*, 11 March 2015, viewed 24 November 2017, <http://www.dailynk.com/english/read.php?cataId=nk02501&num=12966>.

Cumings, Bruce, 'This is what's really behind North Korea's nuclear provocations', *The Nation*, 23 March 2017, viewed 12 November 2017, <https://www.thenation.com/article/this-is-whats-really-behind-north-koreas-nuclear-provocations/>.

Das, Krishna and Spicer, Jonathan, 'The SWIFT hack: how the New York Fed fumbled over the Bangladesh Bank cyber-heist', *Reuters*, 21 July 2016, viewed 24 November 2017, <http://www.reuters.com/investigates/special-report/cyber-heist-federal/>.

Dela Paz, Chrisee, 'Timeline: Tracing the $81-million stolen fund from Bangladesh Bank', *Rappler*, 17 March 2016, viewed 24 November 2017, <https://www.rappler.com/business/industries/209-banking-and-financial-services/125999-timeline-money-laundering-bangladesh-bank>.

Denney, Steven, 'North Korean nationalism: lessons from Pyongyang', *SinoNK*, 8 June 2016, viewed 24 November 2017, <http://sinonk.com/2016/06/08/north-korean-nationalism-lessons-from-pyongyang/>.

Devnath, Arun and Riley, Michael, 'Bangladesh Bank heist probe said to find three hacker groups', *Bloomberg Technology*, 10 May 2016, viewed 24 November 2017, <https://www.bloomberg.com/news/articles/2016-05-10/bangladesh-bank-heist-probe-said-to-find-three-groups-of-hackers>.

Dominguez, Jorge I., 'The perfect dictatorship? Comparing authoritarian rule in South Korea and in Argentina, Brazil, Chile, and Mexico', presented at the Annual Meeting of the American Political Science Association, Boston, 29 August – 1 September 2002, viewed 24 November 2017, <https://wcfia.harvard.edu/files/wcfia/files/690_theperfectdictatorship.pdf>.

The Economist, 'Miscalculating the cost of unification', *Business Insider*, 7 December 2014, viewed 24 November 2017, <http://uk.businessinsider.com/miscalculating-the-cost-of-unification-2014-12>.

Ernsberger Jr., Richard, 'Interview: Melinda Pash, Why is Korea the "Forgotten War"?', *American History Magazine*, 31 March 2014, viewed 24 November 2017, <http://www.historynet.com/interview-melinda-pash-why-is-korea-the-forgotten-war.htm>.

Feffer, John and Gershman, John, 'Fearful symmetry: Washington and Pyongyang', *Institute for Policy Studies,* 1 July 2003, viewed 10 November 2017, <https://www.ips-dc.org/fearful_symmetry_washington_and_pyongyang/>.

Fifield, Anna, 'Life under Kim Jong Un', *The Washington Post,* 17 November 2017, viewed 24 November 2017, https://www.washingtonpost.com/graphics/2017/world/north-korea-defectors/

Gady, F.-S., 'Is North Korea fighting for Assad in Syria?', *The Diplomat,* 24 March 2016, viewed 9 November 2017, <https://thediplomat.com/2016/03/is-north-korea-fighting-for-assad-in-syria/>.

Gregg, Donald, 'Park Chung Hee', *TIME*, 23 August 1999, viewed 24 November 2017, <http://content.time.com/time/world/article/0,8599,2054405,00.html>.

Haggard, S., Jung, E. and Melton, A., 'Is China subsidizing the DPRK? Part one: food', Peterson Institute for International Economics, 29 May 2013, viewed 23 November 2017, <http://blogs.piie.com/nk/?p=10488>.

Harris, Bryan, 'Unveiling the North Korean economy, by Byung-Yeon Kim', *Financial Times*, 4 September 2017, viewed 27 November 2017, <https://www.ft.com/content/2de06fec-8d6a-11e7-9084-d0c17942ba93>.

He, Jun and Xu, Jianchu, 'Is there decentralization in North Korea? Evidence and lessons from the sloping land management program 2004–2014', *Land Use Policy*, vol. 61, 2017, pp. 113–25, <http://dx.doi.org/10.1016/j.landusepol.2016.11.020>.

Hern, Alex and Gibbs, Samuel, 'What is WannaCry ransomware and why is it attacking global computers?', *The Guardian*, 12 May 2017, viewed 24 November 2017, <https://www.theguardian.com/technology/2017/may/12/nhs-ransomware-cyber-attack-what-is-wanacrypt0r-20>.

Hersh, Seymour M., 'The cold test', *The New Yorker,* 27 January 2003, viewed 10 November 2017, <https://www.newyorker.com/magazine/2003/01/27/the-cold-test>.

Hojunester, 'What is minjok?', blog, 1 December 2012, viewed 24 November 2017, <https://hojunester.wordpress.com/2012/12/01/what-is-korean-identity/>.

Human Rights Watch, 'North Korea: events of 2016', 2017, viewed 24 November 2017, <https://www.hrw.org/world-report/2017/country-chapters/north-korea>.

'The Interview: a guide to the cyber attack on Hollywood', *BBC*, 29 December 2014, viewed 24 November 2017, <http://www.bbc.co.uk/news/entertainment-arts-30512032>.

Katona-Apte, J. and Mokdad, A., 'Malnutrition of children in the Democratic People's Republic of North Korea', *Journal of Nutrition*, vol. 128, no. 8, 1998, pp. 1315–19.

Kennedy, John F., 'Joint statement following discussions with chairman Chung Hee Park of Korea', 14 November 1961, online by Gerhard Peters and John T. Woolley, *The American Presidency Project*, viewed 24 November 2017, <http://www.presidency.ucsb.edu/ws/?pid=8442>.

'The Kim family tree: a family firm', *TIME*, 2016, viewed 24 November 2017, <http://content.time.com/time/interactive/0,31813,2107093,00.html>.

Kim Young Sik, 'Who were the Soviet Koreans? The left–right confrontation in Korea – its origin', *Association for Asian Research*, 11 May 2003, viewed 24 November 2017, <http://www.asianresearch.org/articles/1632.html>.

Kono, Yohei, *Statement by the Chief Cabinet Secretary Yohei Kono on the result of the study on the issue of 'comfort women'*, Ministry of Foreign Affairs of Japan, 4 August 1993, viewed 12 November 2017, <https://web.archive.org/web/20140709022903/http:/www.mofa.go.jp/policy/women/fund/state9308.html>.

Korea Konsult, *Mt Paektu – the birthplace of Korean revolution*, viewed 12 November 2017, <http://www.koreakonsult.com/Attraction_Paektu_eng.html>.

Koshino, Yuka, 'Q&A: how much do US military bases in Japan and Korea cost?', *The Wall Street Journal*, 28 April 2016, viewed 24 November 2017, <https://www.wsj.com/articles/q-a-how-much-do-u-s-military-bases-in-japan-and-korea-cost-1461822624>.

Kwak, Rose. 'What do North Koreans do for fun?', *Korea Economic Institute of America*, 2017, viewed 24 November 2017, <http://keia.org/what-do-north-koreans-do-fun>.

Lee, Grace, 'The political philosophy of juche', *Stanford Journal of East Asian Affairs*, vol. 3, no. 1, 2003, viewed 24 November 2017, <https://s3.amazonaws.com/berkley-center/030101LeePoliticalPhilosophyJuche.pdf>.

Mateer, Noelle, 'A rare look inside everyday North Korea', *That's Shanghai,* 28 October 2015, viewed 24 November 2017, <http://www.thatsmags.com/shanghai/post/11417/lit-fest-everyday-north-korea>.

'Missing IT expert Zoha back home', *The Daily Star,* 24 March 2016, viewed 24 November 2017, <http://www.thedailystar.net/frontpage/missing-it-expert-zoha-back-home-1198780>.

Mizan, Habibullah, '13 BB staff guilty of negligence, says CID', *the independent,* 27 August 2016, viewed 24 November 2017, <http://www.theindependentbd.com/printversion/details/57699>.

Oppenheim, Maya, 'What it's like to be a teenager in North Korea', *Independent,* 9 September 2016, viewed 24 November 2017, <http://www.independent.co.uk/news/people/north-korea-independence-day-dating-love-sex-drinking-video-games-and-being-gay-in-north-korea-life-a7233526.html>.

Osnos, Evan, 'The risk of nuclear war with North Korea', *The New Yorker,* 18 September 2017, viewed 24 November 2017, <https://www.newyorker.com/magazine/2017/09/18/the-risk-of-nuclear-war-with-north-korea>.

'North Korea: "no apology" for S Korea Cheonan sinking', *BBC News,* 24 March 2015, viewed 24 November 2017, <http://www.bbc.co.uk/news/world-asia-32013750>.

Papri, Jesmin, 'Bangladesh seeks information about possible North Korea link to cyber heist', *BenarNews,* 24 March 2017, viewed 9 November 2017, <http://www.benarnews.org/english/news/bengali/heist-update-03242017161218.html>.

Park, Ju-min and Pearson, James, 'In North Korea, hackers are a handpicked, pampered elite', *Reuters,* 5 December 2014, viewed 24 November 2017, <http://uk.reuters.com/article/us-sony-cybersecurity-northkorea/in-north-korea-hackers-are-a-handpicked-pampered-elite-idUSKCN0JJ08B20141205>.

Pham, Sherisse, 'Russia just gave North Korea's internet a big boost', *CNN Tech*, 2 October 2017, viewed 24 November 2017, <http://money.cnn.com/2017/10/02/technology/north-korea-russia-internet-link/index.html>.

Powell, Bill and McGirk, Tim, 'The man who sold the bomb', *TIME*, 6 February 2005, viewed 24 November 2017, <content.time.com/time/magazine/article/0,9171,1025193,00.html>.

Prince, Brian, 'South Korea cyber attack tied to DarkSeoul crew: Symantec', *Security Week*, 27 June 2013, viewed 24 November 2017, <http://www.securityweek.com/south-korea-cyber-attack-tied-darkseoul-crew-symantec>.

Quardir, Serajul, 'Bangladesh Bank exposed hackers by cheap switches, no firewall: police', *Reuters*, 21 April 2016, viewed 24 November 2017, <https://www.reuters.com/article/us-usa-fed-bangladesh/bangladesh-bank-exposed-to-hackers-by-cheap-switches-no-firewall-police-idUSKCN0XI1UO>.

Ramani, Samuel, 'The long history of the Pakistan–North Korea nexus', *The Diplomat*, 30 August 2016, viewed 24 November 2017, <https://thediplomat.com/2016/08/the-long-history-of-the-pakistan-north-korea-nexus/>.

Riddle, Lincoln, 'The Korean War – a war of many names', *War History Online*, 16 June 2017, viewed 24 November 2017, <https://www.warhistoryonline.com/korean-war/10-top-facts-the-korean-war-m.html>.

Rogers, Marc, 'The Sony saga: 10 reasons why the FBI is wrong', *ITProPortal*, 22 December 2014, viewed 24 November 2017, <https://www.itproportal.com/2014/12/22/10-pieces-evidence-suggest-sony-pictures-hack-done-north-korea/>.

Ruediger, Frank, 'Economic sanctions and the nuclear issue: lessons from North Korean trade', *38North*, 18 September 2017, viewed 24 November 2017, <http://www.38north.org/2017/09/rfrank091817/>.

Ryan, Rowena, 'The mysterious fake town on North Korea's border', *News.com.au*, 11 July 2014, viewed 24 November 2017, <http://nypost.com/2014/07/11/the-mysterious-fake-town-on-north-koreas-border/>.

Sanger, David, 'Threats and responses: alliances; in North Korea and Pakistan, deep roots of nuclear barter', *The New York Times*, 24 November 2002, viewed 24 November 2017, <http://www.nytimes.com/2002/11/24/world/threats-responses-alliances-north-korea-pakistan-deep-roots-nuclear-barter.html>.

Sanger, David E. and Fackler, Martin, 'NSA breached North Korean networks before Sony attack, officials say', *The New York Times*, 18 January 2015, viewed 24 November 2017, <https://www.nytimes.com/2015/01/19/world/asia/nsa-tapped-into-north-korean-networks-before-sony-attack-officials-say.html?_r=1>.

Sanger, David E. and Broad, William J., 'Trump inherits a secret cyberwar against North Korean missiles', *The New York Times,* 4 March 2017, viewed 10 November 2017, <https://www.nytimes.com/2017/03/04/world/asia/north-korea-missile-program-sabotage.html?_r=0>.

Schneier, Bruce, 'More data on attributing the Sony attack', *Schneier on Security*, 31 December 2014, viewed 24 November 2017, <https://www.schneier.com/blog/archives/2014/12/more_data_on_at.html>.

Shi, Ting and Tweed, David, 'China and Russia warn the US not to seek North Korean regime change', *Bloomberg Politics*, 12 September 2017, viewed 24 November 2017, <https://www.bloomberg.com/news/articles/2017-09-12/in-sanctioning-kim-china-and-russia-warn-u-s-no-regime-change>.

'Sony hacking scandal: execs convinced it's an inside job', *TMZ*, 17 December 2014, viewed 24 November 2017, <http://www.tmz.com/2014/12/17/sony-hack-inside-job-north-korea-investigation/>.

'South Korea history timeline', *World Atlas*, 7 April 2017, viewed 27 November 2017, <http://www.worldatlas.com/webimage/countrys/asia/southkorea/krtimeln.htm>.

'South Korea – timeline', *BBC*, 11 May 2017, viewed 27 November 2017, <http://www.bbc.com/news/world-asia-pacific-15292674>.

Talmadge, Eric, 'North Korea, cyberattacks and "Lazarus": what we really know', *Phys.org*, 2 June 2017, viewed 9 November 2017, <https://phys.org/news/2017-06-north-korea-cyberattacks-lazarus.html>.

Tertitskiy, Fyodor, 'Life in North Korea – the early years', *The Guardian*, 21 December 2015, viewed 24 November 2017, <https://www.theguardian.com/world/2015/dec/21/life-in-north-korea-the-early-years#img-2>.

UCLA International Institute, *Treaty of Annexation: Annexation of Korea by Japan, August 22, 1910*, 10 December 2004, viewed 12 November 2017, <http://international.ucla.edu/institute/article/18447>.

Waterhouse, James and Doble, Anna, 'Bureau 121: North Korea's elite hackers and a "tasteful" hotel in China', *BBC*, 29 May 2015, viewed 24 November 2017, <http://www.bbc.co.uk/newsbeat/article/32926248/bureau-121-north-koreas-elite-hackers-and-a-tasteful-hotel-in-china>.

Audiovisual

Counting the Cost: N Korea unfazed by talks of increasing sanctions, Al Jazeera English, 9 September 2017, viewed 24 November 2017, <https://www.youtube.com/watch?v=RCZo-muQuso>.

The Happiest People on Earth. North Korea: Rulers, Citizens, and Official Narrative, 2 July 2017, RT, viewed 24 November 2017, <https://www.youtube.com/watch?v=7ZMB_TxyuNM>.

Inside North Korea, part 2/3, 19 December 2011, VICE Travel, viewed 24 November 2017, <https://www.youtube.com/ watch?annotation_id=annotation_448028&feature=iv&index=2 &list=PL10943F1A08C72A17&src_vid=24R8JObNNQ4 &v=xw46Ll-Zy4s>.

Interview with a Chinese Veteran from the Korean War, 22 April 2015, viewed 24 November 2017, <https://www.youtube.com/ watch?v=oGrO4emyZG8>.

Juche Strong, 2013, Rob Montz, Vimeo, viewed 24 November, <https://vimeo.com/65907063>.

Money & Power in North Korea: The Hidden Economy, 2015, NHK Documentary, viewed 27 November 2017, <https://www.youtube. com/watch?v=pKYBu9xIfac>.

North Korean Labor Camps: Part 1 of 7, 19 December 2011, VICE News, viewed 24 November 2017, <https://www.youtube.com/ watch?v=awQDLoOnkdI>.

North Korea Nuclear's Trump Card, 7 October 2017, BBC Panorama, <http://www.bbc.co.uk/programmes/b097m386>.

North Korea Day 5, 3 August 2016, Fun for Louis, viewed 27 November 2017, <https://www.youtube.com/watch? v=efqRUmazxBU&index=5&list=PLKdBO8TXUFBgaqcNC d8xyokjUFEdUu9LU>.

North Korea Uncloaked: The Movie, 2012, C.K. Media Enterprises, viewed 24 November 2017, <https://www.youtube.com/ watch?v=czK6dSRIxZs&list=UUrAPOIeEk_BPcFdpWIDM7dg &index=5>.

North Korea's Dangerous Border: Inside The DMZ [Pt.1], Dena Takruri, 12 September 2017, viewed 24 November 2017, <https:// www.youtube.com/watch?v=a12yniZVGLQ>.

Putin: North Koreans Would Rather Eat Grass Than Give Up Nukes, If They Don't Feel Safe, 6 September 2017, Russia Insider,

viewed 24 November 2017, <https://www.youtube.com/
watch?v=xFedyqandWU>.

Sony Hacking Scandal – Crime of the Year, 18 December 2014,
TheLipTV, viewed 24 November 2017, <https://www.youtube.
com/watch?v=QlKNoZu-UKA>.

*This Is What It's Like Inside North Korea's Luxury Ski Resort | Short
Film Showcase,* National Geographic, 2017, viewed 24 November
2017, <https://www.youtube.com/watch?v=csoP8Didoi0>.

Who Made North Korea a Nuclear Power: Dr A.Q. Khan, or Pakistan?
17 May 2017, Global Conflict, viewed 24 November 2017,
<https://www.youtube.com/watch?v=B7ehXxA5oj4&t=135s>.

Why North Korea Wants Nuclear Weapons, 24 April 2017, Caspian
Report, viewed 24 November 2017, <https://www.youtube.com/
watch?v=ykYRsmIQkyw>.

Why is North Korea in the Axis of Evil? Annabel Park interview with
John Feffer, 18 January 2007, Eric Byler, viewed 24 November
2017, <https://www.youtube.com/watch?v=IEBlFkqIdCo>.

Books
Castells, Manuel, *End of Millennium*, 2nd edn, Blackwell Publishers,
Oxford, 2000.

Chan, Anita, *China's Workers Under Assault: Exploitation and Abuse
in a Globalizing Economy,* Routledge, Abingdon and New York,
2015 [2001].

Collins, Robert, *Marked for Life: Songbun. North Korea's Social
Classification System*, The Committee for Human Rights in North
Korea, Washington, DC, 2012, viewed 24 November 2017,
<https://www.hrnk.org/uploads/pdfs/HRNK_Songbun_Web.
pdf>.

Cumings, Bruce, *Korea's Place in the Sun: A Modern History,* updated
edn, W. W. Norton, New York, 2005 [1997].

Cumings, Bruce, *North Korea: Another Country,* The New Press, New York, 2003.

Dower, John, *Embracing Defeat,* Penguin Press, London, 1999.

Forsberg, Aaron, *America and the Japanese Miracle*, University of North Carolina Press, London, 2000.

Galluppi, Massimo and Mazzei, Franco (eds), *Campania e Cina,* Esi, Naples, 2005.

Jong-Woo, Han and Tae-Hern, Jung (eds), *Understanding North Korea: Indigenous Perspectives*, Lexington Books, Lanham, MD, 2014.

Herbert, Anthony B. and Wooten, James T., *Soldier,* Holt, Rinehart and Winston, New York, 1973.

Hubbard, L. Ron, *Dianetics: The Modern Science of Mental Health,* Bridge Publications, Commerce City, CA, 2007 [1950].

Jacques, Martin, *When China Rules the World,* Allen Lane, London, 2009.

Kim, Byung-Yeon, *Unveiling the North Korean Economy: Collapse and Transition,* Cambridge University Press, Cambridge, 2017.

Kim Hyung-A, *Korea's Development Under Park Chung Hee: Rapid Industrialization, 1961–79*, RoutledgeCurzon, London and New York, 2004.

Kim Jong-il, *Aphorism*, Foreign Language Publishing House, Pyongyang, Juche 103, 2014.

Mazzei, Franco and Volpi, Vittorio, *Asia al Centro* [Asia at the Center], Egea-Università Bocconi Editore, Milan, 2006.

Napoleoni, Loretta, *The Chinese Miracle: A Modern Day Industrial Revolution*, Seven Stories Press, New York, 2012.

Oberdorfer, Don, *The Two Koreas: A Contemporary History*, Basic Books, New York, 2001 [1997].

Rees, David, *Korea: An Illustrated History from Ancient Times to 1945 – Introduction*, Hippocrene Books, New York, NY, 2001.

Tudor, Daniel, *A Geek in Korea: Discovering Asia's New Kingdom of Cool*, Tuttle Publishing, North Clarendon, VT, 2014.

Tudor, Daniel, and Pearson, James, *North Korea Confidential: Private Markets, Fashion Trends, Prison Camps, Dissenters and Defectors*, Tuttle Publishing, North Clarendon, VT, 2015.

Institutional reports

The Bassiouni Group, *Situation Analysis of Children and Women in the Democratic People's Republic of Korea – 2017*, United Nations Children's Fund, Pyongyang, 2016, viewed 24 November 2017, <https://www.unicef.org/dprk/Situation_Analysis_of_Children_ and_Women_in_DPR_Korea_UNICEF_2017.pdf>.

Jiyoon, Kim; Friedoff, Karl; Chungku, Kang and Euicheol, Lee, *South Korean Attitudes Toward North Korea and Reunification*, Asian Public Opinion Report, The Asian Institute for Policy Studies, Seoul, 2015, viewed 24 November 2017, <https://thediplomat.com/wp-content/uploads/2015/01/ thediplomat_2015-01-29_13-53-09.pdf>.

Jun, Jenny; LaFoy, Scott and Sohn, Ethan, *North Korea's Cyber Operations: Strategy and Responses*, Center for Strategic International Studies, Washington, DC, 2015, viewed 27 November 2017, <https://csis-prod.s3.amazonaws.com/s3fs-public/legacy_files/files/ publication/151216_Cha_NorthKoreasCyberOperations_Web. pdf>.

CPSIA information can be obtained
at www.ICGtesting.com
Printed in the USA
LVOW03s0319220118
563397LV00003B/5/P